THE ECONOMIC TIME BOMB

THE ECONOMIC TIME BOMB

How You Can Profit from the Emerging Crises

Harry Browne

ST. MARTIN'S PRESS

New York

DESIGN BY JUDITH A. STAGNITTO

Library of Congress Cataloging-in-Publication Data

Browne, Harry.
    The economic time bomb : how you can profit from the emerging crises / Harry Browne.
        p.   cm.
    ISBN 0-312-02581-5
    1. Investments—United States.   2. United States—Economic conditions—1981–   I. Title.
HG4910.B75 1989
332.6′78—dc19   88-30824
                                                          CIP

10 9 8 7 6 5 4 3 2

to
Pamela

CONTENTS

Epilogue

Appendices

Prologue

1

The Economic
Time Bomb

For the first time in many years, I feel a sense of immediate danger about the economy.

I believe the prosperity we've enjoyed in the 1980s is about to end.

The economy is threatened by three grave problems left over from the turbulent 1970s. These problems were pushed into the background by the prosperity of the 1980s, but they weren't solved. They've been growing more dangerous all the while—ticking away like a time bomb.

Most likely, the three problems will begin to erupt when the next recession arrives—probably in 1989 or 1990. I expect that recession to be severe, and I expect it to revive the destructive pattern of the 1970s—when recessions alternated with inflation that rose to 6%, 12%, and finally 15% at the peak in 1980.

But history never repeats itself too neatly. The troubles of the 1990s will unfold in their own way.

The next decade could be considerably more chaotic than the 1970s, because the economy is already suffering so much of the

3

stress that normally isn't felt until after a recession is well under way. Bankruptcies are widespread in the oil and farming industries, and in some real-estate markets. The capital of commercial banks and savings institutions has already been depleted through loan losses. And federal budget deficits are already well over $100 billion per year.

The federal deficit is set to take off upward. The typical recessionary drop-off in federal revenues could send the deficit to $200 billion or more. A government running so deeply in the red won't have the latitude to try to spend its way out of a recession. If it tries to do so, the budget deficits could balloon to $400 billion, and interest rates would rise above the 20% level reached in 1980.

RECENT HISTORY

Before we look at the three problems that make up the economic time bomb, we need to take a brief look back to see where they came from.

As I'll discuss in Chapter 2, the economy is injured by abrupt changes in the quantity of money in circulation (the total amount of cash we hold). If the supply of money doesn't grow in step with the needs of the economy, commerce is stifled and a recession follows. If money growth *outruns* the needs of the economy, the excess causes inflation—an increase in the general level of prices.

From the end of World War II to the end of the 1950s, growth in the money supply was moderate and somewhat steady. As a result, the 1950s were a period of mild recessions and virtually no inflation.

In the 1960s, the federal government initiated a host of new programs, and its expenditures rose accordingly. The government began running a budget deficit every year—a practice that continues to this day.

The government's growing need for credit tended to push interest rates upward. To counter this, the Federal Reserve System ("the Fed," the government agency responsible for controlling the supply of money) became more active.

The Fed bought large portions of the government's new debt—paying for its purchases of government bonds with newly created money. Money growth, which had been modest and stable for close to two decades, became intense and erratic.

By the end of the 1960s, money creation by the Fed had caused the inflation rate to rise to 5%—which was alarming at the time. In 1969 the Fed saw no choice but to slow down the creation of new money to keep inflation from becoming even worse.

Stuck on the Seesaw

The sharp drop in money growth in 1969 did help dampen inflation, but it also brought on a recession in 1970. When the recession approached a severity not seen since the 1930s, the Federal Reserve panicked and flooded the economy with more new money. This cured the recession, but led to even greater inflation in the mid-1970s—which caused the Fed to restrict monetary growth once again.

And so the economy found itself on an inflation-recession seesaw that swung back and forth throughout the 1970s. Rapid money growth led to inflation—which forced the Fed to cut back money growth severely—which led to a recession—which forced the Fed to create new money even more rapidly—and so on.

Also in the 1960s and 1970s, the government was expanding its influence over all sectors of the economy.

The government imposed new regulations on business in the name of product safety, justice for employees, civil rights, the environment, public health, the war in Vietnam, the war on inflation, the war on drugs, the war on OPEC, and any other problem—real or imaginary—that any politician wanted to fix.

Government spending rose at a fast clip. Federal deficits became chronic, and automatic spending programs assured that the deficits would grow. By the end of the 1970s the government's budget was over 7 times as large as it had been in 1960.

By 1978, inflation was up to 9% and rising rapidly—the fruit of 18 years of stop-and-go monetary growth. The Federal Reserve could break out of the pattern only by imposing severe limits on money growth for several years in a row—which would surely bring on a recession worse than the government and the public would tolerate.

The economy was dancing toward destruction, and there didn't seem to be any way to stop the music.

A New Direction

But it did stop.

In 1978 the Federal Reserve System, deeply worried about rising inflation, announced a new policy of slow, stable money growth—similar to what had prevailed in the 1950s. Of course, by 1978 the Fed had adopted and abandoned new policies so many times that this one was received skeptically.

But, in fact, the Federal Reserve stuck to this new policy long enough to make it work. Growth in the money supply fell to a modest rate, and stayed there. As expected, the sharp change led to a recession in 1980, but the Fed held firm. And it didn't panic when the economy continued to weaken and an even worse recession began in mid-1981.

Because it held firm, the Fed won a victory. Inflation fell steeply—from a high of 15% in early 1980 to 2% in 1983.

The times were changing on another front as well. Ronald Reagan became president in 1981, and he was able to get a major reduction in tax rates through Congress. Those tax cuts helped the economy weather the 1981–82 recession and, together with the further cuts enacted in 1986, made the 1980s a period of wide-spread prosperity.

The election of Ronald Reagan also promised a fundamental

change in government. Most people assumed that government would become smaller and intrude less into the economy. The prospect of less government intervention eased the fear that inflation would return, and encouraged the expansion of the economy.

Having reached the other side of the 1981–82 recession, we had a fresh start—a chance for a recession-free and inflation-free economy. The Federal Reserve needed only to continue with the stable policy it had begun in 1978.

Federal deficits could have become a thing of the past. Starting in late 1982, the economy grew rapidly—and so did the government's tax revenues, despite (or because of) lower tax rates. If government spending were held to a modest increase each year, the rising revenue would soon catch up with spending.

There still were weak spots in the economy, but the climate for fixing them was ideal. Deregulation was in vogue, and within sight was a freer, more prosperous economy that could readily handle its problems.

Paradise Lost

But the government threw it all away.

In late 1982 the Federal Reserve once again turned on its money machine—even though the worst of the recession was over. The Fed abandoned its policy of steady money growth, and since then has given the country the same stop-and-go money policy that was its trademark in the 1970s.

And the government spent all the new tax revenue that prosperity could generate—so that the deficits not only remained, they expanded. Ronald Reagan, who had worked so hard to get the tax cuts through Congress, seemed to lose interest in the rest of his economic program. He gave up his goal of restricting the size of government—confining himself instead to cutting a billion dollars here or there from congressional spending programs.

At great cost, the economy had managed to escape from the

inflation-recession seesaw. And the tax cuts had unleashed a new prosperity that was powerful enough to solve all the remaining economic problems.

But the government wasted the opportunity.

THREE PROBLEMS

What was done created the prosperity of the 1980s. What was left undone assured that the prosperity would be temporary.

Three severe problems have continued to grow along with the economy. Any one of them could erupt into a runaway crisis at any time.

1. The Inflation-Recession Seesaw

The first problem is the behavior of the Federal Reserve System. The Fed has resumed the erratic monetary policy that so disturbed the economy in the 1970s.

Since mid-1982, the Fed has been creating new money in a chaotic, fast-and-slow pattern. The money supply increased by 12% in 1985, by 17% in 1986, and then by only 3% in 1987. By switching from one extreme to the other, the Fed assured the worst of all worlds—the stock market crash of 1987, rising inflation in 1987–88, and a recession in 1989 or 1990.[1]

Because of the dangerous size of the federal deficit, and because of the fragile state of the banking system, we can expect the Fed to spare no paper and ink in getting us out of the next recession. The new money the Fed produces will assure severe inflation down the road—perhaps by 1991 or 1992.

[1]The money growth figures are for the M1 definition of the money supply. M2 rose 8% in 1985, 9% in 1986, and only 4% in 1987.

Because the connection between monetary policy and the economy is critical, we'll examine it in more detail in Chapter 2.

2. Federal Deficits

The second growing problem is the government's annual budget deficit.

Throughout the 1980s we heard forecasts that the federal debt would lead to skyrocketing interest rates or runaway inflation. Because the predictions didn't pan out, the deficits no longer seem to be an urgent problem.

But, as we'll see in Chapter 3, the government's need for credit, already enormous, may soon go up sharply. That would push interest rates—on mortgages, consumer credit, bonds, and business loans—into the stratosphere. Many people will be forced to decide against borrowing at all. But the government, with a mountain of debt to be refinanced each year, won't have that choice.

Higher interest rates will increase the government's borrowing costs, at the same time that a credit-starved economy is generating smaller tax revenues—magnifying the deficit.

Once government borrowing dominates the credit markets, government debt will feed on itself: larger deficits push interest rates upward—which makes the government's borrowing costs larger and its tax revenues smaller—which causes the deficits to be larger still. In short, a vicious circle.

The only question is *when* government borrowing will reach the lift-off stage. There's good reason to think the day is fast approaching.

A prosperous, low-inflation economy has been able to finance the deficits up to now. But that good fortune merely encouraged the government to put off dealing with the deficit. The next recession will change everything: with the government already so deeply in the red, falling tax revenues and automatic spending increases could produce deficits that overwhelm the credit markets.

We'll look at the deficits in detail in Chapter 3.

3. Weakness in the Banking System

The third problem is the weak condition of most banks. The troubled banks are approaching a crisis that will affect you and me and every other bank customer directly.

Many banks have a smaller net worth than you do. If they tried to pay off all their depositors, they would have very little money left—and many banks would run out of money before everyone was paid. If you're the last in line at the bank, you could have a very long wait.

A resumption of high rates of inflation could be the shock that sets off a banking crisis. Inflation would force banks to pay much higher interest rates to keep deposits—even though many of their customers would still be paying the bank lower, fixed rates on long-term loans. Or a severe recession, with more bad loans for the banks to write off, could be the trigger. In either situation, the banks would exhaust the little capital they have left.

The ensuing wave of bank failures would be many times too large for the Federal Deposit Insurance Corporation (FDIC) to handle. When the FDIC's reserves run dry, the government will be called upon to replenish them. But in the middle of a deep recession or rising inflation, the government would already be hundreds of billions of dollars in the red—even if it turns down other requests for aid. Facing its own debt crisis, it's not likely that the government will provide 100% of everything that's asked of it.

We'll explore the banking problems further in Chapter 4.

READY TO EXPLODE

These three problems—the erratic monetary policy, the federal deficits, and the near-insolvency of so many banks—are separate problems. But they feed on one another; when one explodes, they all will explode. And anything done to buy time for one problem will aggravate the other two.

The problems began to take shape in the 1960s. They contributed to the turbulence of the 1970s, and—except for the brief monetary reform in the early 1980s—they've continued to worsen without letup.

Together they are an economic time bomb. The bomb is ticking toward the day when one of the problems slips out of control and beyond the government's ability to postpone the day of reckoning.

The 1980s have been a welcome intermission. The steady monetary policy of 1978–82 created an ideal climate for the tax cuts of 1981–83 to work their magic.

The economy got a second wind with the passage of even larger tax-rate reductions in 1986. These cuts took effect in 1987 and 1988, and they're probably the main reason the economy continued to confound the recurring forecasts of recession.

In Chapter 6 we'll examine the power of low tax rates to protect the economy. And we'll see how a tax increase could remove that protection and set off the economic time bomb.

Except for a possible cut in capital-gain rates, tax rates now are as low as they're likely to go. From here on, a tax increase is more likely than a further cut.

Vulnerability to Shocks

Throughout the 1980s, the economy has been vulnerable to any shock that might set off one of the three problems.

The shock could have been a major new program piled onto the federal budget, or anything that sent interest rates high enough to drive more banks over the edge, or any government scheme harmful enough to send the economy into a recession.

There were plenty of proposals that might have provided such a shock. They included plans:

- to raise taxes;
- to interfere with foreign trade, which would halt the inflow of needed foreign capital, hurt America's export business, and deprive many American companies of needed supplies from abroad;
- to bail out failing banks and savings & loans, which would add tens of billions of dollars to the federal budget;
- to impose new regulations on the stock market, which would discourage new investment in the economy;
- to force businessmen to pay for the social prejudices of politicians, through "comparable worth" schemes or the banning of essential minerals from South Africa;
- to impose mandatory health-care programs on business, which would run costs and prices upward, reduce wages, and discourage investment.

In Chapters 5 through 9, we'll look at the consequences of such programs, and at the merits of the ideas behind them. But, of course, these proposals are only examples. The government crusade that actually sets off the time bomb may be one we haven't even heard of yet.

Most of the proposals try to fix something that isn't broken, such as the foreign trade balance. Or, when directed at a real problem, like the federal deficit or the weakness in the banking system, the medicine prescribed is poisonous.

Some of the proposals are more dangerous than others. The economy might have tolerated any of them 20 or 30 years ago. But not now.

Presidential Politics

During most of the past eight years, such proposals have been stillborn. Either they were vetoed by the president or they were left to die in Congress because a veto had been promised.

As the Reagan administration staggered to a close, the president's determination to protect the economy from Congress seemed to flag. He had backed off earlier from trying to reduce government spending, and in the final years he surrendered on many other issues.

But for the most part, he did prevent Congress from increasing income tax rates, imposing new regulations on the investment markets or the economy, starting expensive new programs, or enacting a harsh trade bill.[2]

And he held the line despite constant pressure from Congress and the press to "do something" about the unprecedented budget deficits, the trade deficits, and the stock market crash.

But now there's a new president—one with more energy and ambition than Ronald Reagan had, and not nearly so determined to protect the economy from the government.

We now must fear that a bold new program of some kind will be pushed into law by a president eager to demonstrate that he's in charge—a program that will speed up the clock on the economic time bomb.

Rising Interest Rates

The three problems are setting us up for an era of unusually high interest rates that could bring the economy almost to a dead stop and cause disarray in the investment markets.

[2]A trade bill did pass in 1988. But, apart from a few of its provisions, it was a toothless tiger that allowed congressmen to talk tough without doing much damage to international trade.

Interest yields on newly issued bonds could rise to 20% or more—causing prices of existing bonds to drop through the floor. For stock dividends to provide the same percentage yields as bonds, the Dow Jones Industrial Average would need to fall below 1000.

Your bank account might not survive such a crisis. And money market funds that rely on bank certificates of deposit—which means most money market funds—would be no safer.

TIME TO BE CONCERNED AGAIN

In *How You Can Profit from the Coming Devaluation,* in 1970, I wrote about the inflationary problems I saw brewing. I tried to arm readers against those problems—and to show them how to profit from the situation.

You Can Profit from a Monetary Crisis in 1974 warned that the turmoil was far from over. And *New Profits from the Monetary Crisis* in 1978 tried to prepare readers for a change from the inflationary 1970s.

I've been more subdued during the 1980s—partly because my investment strategy should provide safety and profit in good times or bad, and partly because I saw no immediate cause for alarm. I wouldn't have been shocked if the three problems had erupted into crises, but I saw no sign that they were about to.

The situation today is different. Although the future is always uncertain, the chance of disaster now is much greater—in fact, too great to ignore or to keep quiet about.

The three problems are approaching the limit of manageability, and the new administration may stumble across that limit. We're in trouble, and I doubt that either President Bush or Congress has a realistic solution in mind.

I feel very strongly that you *must* arrange protection for yourself, and you must do it soon. You might not survive the 1990s if you're invested wholly in stocks or mutual funds, or if you believe some financial guru will get you in and out of the stock market at the right times, or if you believe that holding only gold or Treasury bills is enough to protect you in all circumstances.

I think it's essential that you have an investment program that will protect your savings and your wealth from anything and everything that might happen. If you'll take the day or two necessary to accomplish this, you may never have to worry about the subject again.

The strategy I'll offer won't force you to become a sophisticated investor. You can, on your own, set up an extremely simple, safe program and then walk away from it—confident that it will take care of you no matter how things unfold. Once you've made sure you're safe, you can—*if you wish*—set aside part of your wealth to bet on the crises or on any other speculation that catches your eye.

The economy's problems are serious, but you aren't helpless— no matter how large or small your wealth may be, no matter how little or much you know about investments, and even though *no one* can be sure exactly how the future will unfold. In Part II, I'll show how you can take care of yourself.

If, anywhere in the book, you come across a word you don't understand, check the glossary beginning on page 271; most key words used in the book are defined there. And if you can't remember where you saw some point, there's an extensive index in the back of the book.

CRISES ARE IN

A number of crisis books have been published in the past few years—especially since the 1987 stock market crash. In fact, there may be more crisis books around now than there were during the crisis-ridden 1970s.

Every one I've read maintains that there's one, and only one, possible future ahead of us. And it invites you to follow the author down the barrel of his chosen cannon. Of course, he tells you that he's never ever been wrong before. But if his lucky streak stops now, you could lose your life savings. If that approach has frightened you more than the potential crises themselves, I don't blame you.

In addition, the 1980s have seen plenty of experts cry "Wolf!" Despite their cries, we haven't seen $5-per-gallon gasoline, or runaway inflation from the federal deficits, or a recession following the stock market crash, or any of the events foreseen in the many authoritative predictions.

So I can understand if you don't take *any* warning seriously.

But I hope you'll stick with me through this short book. Even if we don't agree about everything, you may gain a better understanding of the banking crisis, a new perspective on the foreign trade deficit, a different view of the publicized stock market scandals, or a new way of thinking about your investments.

I won't ask you to bet your savings on what I believe. Instead, I'll offer a realistic plan that will shield you from *whatever* happens—while allowing you to profit for however long the economy holds together.

So let's get started.

PART I

The
Emerging Crises

2

The Monetary Crisis

Whatever the problem might be, the government has a simple solution: hand out some money.

Whether the problem is unemployment, penniless farmers, banks in trouble, weak national defense, a drought, an epidemic, or an increase in UFO sightings, the government knows only one remedy: pass the money around.

For the most part, the government acquires the money it hands out by collecting taxes and by borrowing. But there's one problem the government can't treat with money it gets from taxing or borrowing—and that's the problem of a recession.

A recession is a slowing in the general level of business activity. More products, services, and labor are for sale than people feel able to buy. The results are business failures, loan defaults, and unemployment.

To put it more simply, there just isn't enough money to go around. People don't have enough cash to be willing to buy all the goods for sale and employ all the people looking for work.

The government can't treat a recession by taxing or borrowing, because those methods don't increase the total amount of money available to the economy as a whole. Taxing and borrowing merely take money from one person (the taxpayer or the lender) and deliver it to another (the beneficiary of a government program).

For the government to stimulate the economy and cure a recession, it must spend money that comes literally from nowhere. It must be brand-new money—money that increases the total nationwide supply of cash. Only new money adds to the purchasing power of some people without simultaneously reducing the purchasing power of others.

The idea may sound fanciful, but the government really does spend money that's created out of thin air. It has the power to print as much money as it sees fit, and it does exactly that.

CONSEQUENCES OF MONEY CREATION

Spending new money is the answer to a politician's prayer. The people who receive the new money are grateful, and no one else has to pay for it. The pleasant consequences are immediate and obvious; the bad consequences are delayed and seemingly unrelated.

But the bad consequences far outweigh the pleasant ones. Four problems flow from the practice of solving problems by printing money.

1. Price Inflation

First, creating too much new money causes inflation—a rise in the general level of prices. When anything becomes more plentiful, its value tends to drop—and money is no exception.

Everyone who receives a share of the new money competes more vigorously for the existing supply of goods and services. Eventually (usually within one to three years), prices in general are pushed higher than they would have been without the new money.

2. Subsidizing Failure

New money is created and spent to prevent a recession or to end one. To succeed in its purpose, the new money must rescue business projects that otherwise would fail. But many of those products, services, and companies are failing because consumers in general would rather spend their money on something else. Rescuing them means keeping mistakes alive.

People do make mistakes. Sometimes they build factories that produce goods that too few consumers are willing to pay for. Sometimes people design products that cost more to make than customers ordinarily are willing to pay. Sometimes companies fail to keep up with changes in technology or changes in the needs and tastes of their customers. Sometimes a business produces the right product the right way at the right price—but produces too much of it.

A recession compels the manager of a company that's taken a wrong turn to face up to his mistake. He's forced to acknowledge that at least some portion of the land, facilities, materials, labor, and talent the business uses could yield more of what consumers want if those resources were used differently.

And he's forced to act on that information. He has to free up resources for other, more profitable uses—by dropping a product, or changing the way he makes it, or producing it at a slower rate.

But an influx of new money encourages people to buy more of almost everything temporarily—and so the truth is hidden from company managers. The new money allows wasteful errors to continue and allows dying companies to survive a little longer. It tells the businessman who has made a mistake to keep making it.

3. Habit-Forming

The injection of new money prolongs the lives of companies, industries, and products that consumers otherwise wouldn't support. When the effect of the new money wears off, all the questionable projects that had been rescued will need help again.[1]

When the marginal projects falter again, the government will have to print even more new money, in order to prevent another recession. But the stimulative effect of new money never lasts for long, so the government will be drawn to the printing press again and again.

4. Escalating

The doses of new money, to succeed in their purpose, must become larger and larger—which is why inflation can destroy an economy, not merely disturb it.

In an economy with stable prices, almost *any* quantity of new money will have a stimulative effect. But if prices are rising at, say, 4% per year, a 4% increase in available cash will have little effect—since the new money will be barely enough to permit people to buy what they were buying a year ago. To add to total purchasing power, the new money must *more* than compensate for price inflation.

Because each dose of new money leads to higher prices down the road, it guarantees that the next dose will have to be larger to keep the economy afloat. If inflation has been pushed up to, say, 4%, it may take a 6% dose of new money to fend off a recession. But that will lead after a while to still greater inflation—say, 6%. Then the next dose of new money will have to be substantially *greater* than 6% to have an impact.

Every time the dose is increased, inflation becomes worse. Every time inflation becomes worse, the minimum dose of new money needed to stimulate the economy becomes greater.

Of course, the government could stop at any time—just by ceasing to create new money. But then all the mistaken projects it

[1]Of course, there are examples of companies—such as Chrysler—that were aided by the government and then succeeded on their own. But those examples are remembered for the very reason that they are exceptional—not because they're the norm.

had kept alive would come tumbling down at one time. The government would bring on a recession much worse than the one it tried to avoid in the first place. It could even bring on a depression.

And it isn't just the weak that are hurt when the government stops printing new money. It's everyone who has planned his affairs on the assumption that inflation would continue. Well-run companies are ruined because they committed themselves to automatic pay raises, or because they borrowed at high interest rates that looked cheap when inflation was soaring. And almost all companies are hurt because so many of their customers are in trouble or worried about the future.

As with drugs, it's easy to say "no" the first time the government considers creating new money. But after saying "yes" a few times, the fixes need to be larger and larger to have any effect, and it becomes harder and harder to resist the temptation. Once an economy has become hooked on inflation, it can't avoid the painful withdrawal of a deep recession. And if inflation has gone too far, the cost of a cure is a depression.

And if the addiction isn't cured, eventually it is fatal. There simply is no built-in limit to the addiction. Inflation peaked at 15% in 1980, but that doesn't mean 15% would be the limit in the 1990s. The next peak might be 20% or 25%. And double-digit inflation can become triple-digit inflation.

Streams of Money

In practice, new money isn't created in distinct doses. It streams into the economy continuously. The government regulates the stream—deciding almost daily how much new money the economy needs.

When it issues too little, the economy tends to slow down. When it issues about what the economy needs, the economy purrs along. When it issues too much, inflation follows.

Regulating the stream to issue just the right amount is a tricky business, and it goes wrong more often than not. The government doesn't know in advance the effect a given increase in the supply of money will have. Both the effect on price inflation and the time that will pass before the effect takes hold are unpredictable. The government has to guess—and hope.

The government must work in the dark because the impact of new money depends on just how much cash people want to hold in reserve rather than spend immediately. The more money people want to hold, the more new money the economy can absorb without causing inflation. But when the new money is more than people want to hold, the money is spent almost immediately, moves quickly from hand to hand, and pushes up prices.

Attitudes can't be measured precisely, and they are always changing. If people feel that tough times may be coming, they may—in general—want to hold a greater amount of money inactive and in reserve for a rainy day. If they feel relatively comfortable about the future, they probably will be willing to hold less and spend more.

If they expect inflation in the near future, they will want to hold even less money. Whatever they plan to buy, they will be inclined to buy soon—before prices go higher.

If people fear rapid inflation, they may even borrow heavily to buy now what they might want later. Combined with a reluctance to save money that's depreciating, this tends to drive interest rates upward in an inflationary period.

And when inflation subsides, or is expected to subside, it becomes more attractive to hold cash in reserve—rather than spend it quickly.

HISTORY OF MONEY CREATION

From the beginning of the republic until 1913, the government never tried to provide the "right" amount of money. New money came into circulation when it was issued by private banks, or when individuals deposited gold at the U.S. Treasury.

No one thought the supply of money was a tool with which to manipulate the economy. Even when the U.S. government issued the Civil War "greenbacks," the purpose was to finance a war, not to fight a recession.

The Federal Reserve System

In 1913 everything changed. The government created the Federal Reserve System and charged it with the task of assuring a stable economy and a stable price level. It was to accomplish this by maintaining an "elastic currency"—a supply of money that would be expanded or contracted to fit the needs of commerce.

The system consists of 12 Federal Reserve Banks, supervised by a Board of Governors who are appointed by the President of the United States. The Federal Reserve Banks are banks for bankers. A commercial bank keeps money on deposit at a Federal Reserve Bank to facilitate payments to and from other banks.

As a matter of practice, the Federal Reserve (the Fed) creates new money by buying U.S. Treasury bonds from one of the large commercial banks (such as Bank of America or Chase Manhattan Bank) that operates as a bond dealer. The Fed pays for a bond purchase by crediting the commercial bank's account at a Reserve Bank.

Because the Fed has very little money of its own, the payment it makes to the commercial bank is created out of nothing. Brand-new money has been added to the economy.

And the dollars are as good as all the other dollars in circulation. The commercial bank can use them to buy investments, to increase its reserves, or to make loans to its customers. If the bank wants actual currency, the Fed will print it and deliver it to the bank's door.

Fed Performance

Since the Federal Reserve was established in 1913, money has been created in an erratic pattern—and that has been a chronic source of trouble for the economy.

One effect is instability in the general level of prices. The graph on page 27 shows the yearly inflation rate in the United States since 1800. We can see that prices have been *less* stable since 1913 (when the Fed was established) than before. Prior to 1913, the yearly inflation rate almost always remained within a range of +5% and −5%, except when the country was at war. But since 1913, peacetime has been no more peaceful than wartime.

The graph on page 28 illustrates the problem in a different way. It shows the history of the U.S. Consumer Price Index (an estimate of the general level of prices in America) from 1800 through 1988. The pattern throughout the 19th century was for periods of rising prices to be followed by periods of falling prices—so that the "normal" price level returned eventually.

But the creation of the Federal Reserve System changed all that. In this century, with only one exception, rising prices have been followed by prices rising further. And the trend has become progressively worse.

Ups & Downs

During World War I, inflation soared to over 15%. Then the price level *dropped* by 10% in the single year of 1921, as the country suffered a brief, but very deep, depression. Of course, it was thought that the Fed had learned enough from the experience to assure that such shocks would never occur again.

But that wasn't the case. The Fed set the money screws too tight in the late 1920s—leading to the stock market crash of 1929. The Fed reacted to the crash by tightening even further—bringing on the Great Depression and a deflation in wages, consumer prices,

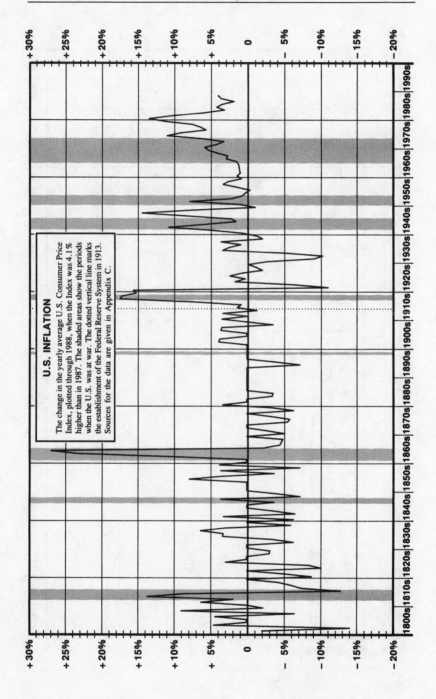

U.S. INFLATION

The change in the yearly average U.S. Consumer Price Index, plotted through 1988, when the Index was 4.1% higher than in 1987. The shaded areas show the periods when the U.S. was at war. The dotted vertical line marks the establishment of the Federal Reserve System in 1913. Sources for the data are given in Appendix C.

Ratio Scale

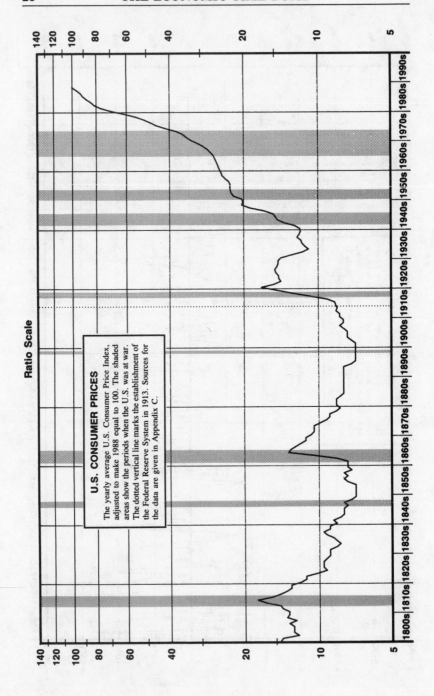

U.S. CONSUMER PRICES

The yearly average U.S. Consumer Price Index, adjusted to make 1988 equal to 100. The shaded areas show the periods when the U.S. was at war. The dotted vertical line marks the establishment of the Federal Reserve System in 1913. Sources for the data are given in Appendix C.

and investments. With other agencies of the government trying to hold wages and prices up, the conflict caused the Depression to drag on throughout the 1930s.

World War II brought inflation of 15%. But by the early 1950s, things had settled down. The government dismantled the war machine, and the Federal Reserve kept money growth very moderate. There was practically no price inflation, recessions were mild, and the economy prospered.

The New Economics

But the direction changed in the 1960s.

Government became more energetic and attempted to use its budget and the Federal Reserve's power to create new money to avoid recessions altogether.

As the graph on page 30 shows, the creation of money increased sharply in the 1960s (from the 1950s' rates) and continued to increase in the 1970s.

As you would expect, this led to an outbreak of inflation. Starting in 1964, the inflation rate moved upward in three broad waves—to peaks of 6% in 1970, 12% in 1974, and 15% in 1980. It was the worst peacetime inflation in American history.[2]

Recessions

Along with the rising waves of inflation came a series of severe recessions.

Whenever the inflation rate rose high enough to worry the Federal Reserve, the Fed would slow, or even stop, its creation of

[2]All references to the price inflation rate are for changes in the U.S. Consumer Price Index over 12-month periods, which are more extreme than the yearly averages shown in the graph on page 27.

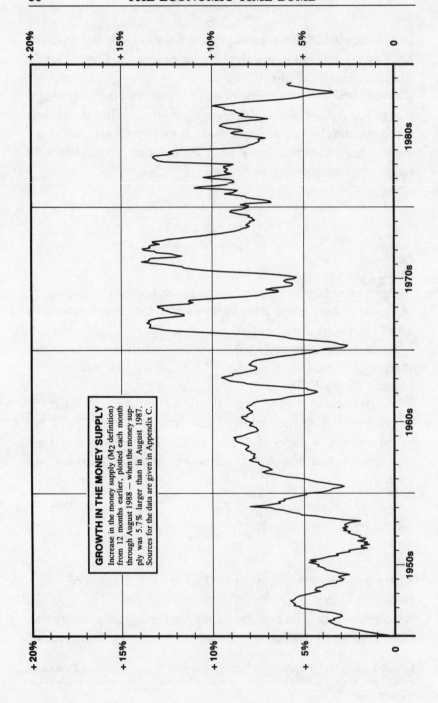

GROWTH IN THE MONEY SUPPLY

Increase in the money supply (M2 definition) from 12 months earlier, plotted each month through August 1988 — when the money supply was 5.7% larger than in August 1987. Sources for the data are given in Appendix C.

new money. The economy would receive *less* money than needed, and a recession would ensue.

The ordeal of tight money would indeed reduce inflation—but not immediately. There's always a delay between the onset of tight money and the slowing of inflation. As a result, the inflation rate usually wouldn't begin falling until the middle of the recession. But by then the Fed would be near panic over the downturn in the economy, and would resume creating new money at a rapid clip—thereby financing the next wave of inflation.

The result was an inflation-recession seesaw, with each swing more violent than the one before.

INFLATION DISAPPEARS

Throughout the 1960s and 1970s, every announcement by the government that inflation had been brought under control was followed by more inflation. So the public had little reason to believe that inflation would ever be licked. This discouraged the public from holding on to the depreciating money—which made it even more difficult for the Fed to bring inflation under control.

In 1978 the Federal Reserve Board chairman vowed that henceforth the creation of new money would be more modest, more stable, and more predictable. Not many people took the announcement seriously—given the Fed's record.

And, in fact, the inflation rate—feeding on previous doses of new money—continued upward, reaching 15% early in 1980.

But then inflation turned downward and kept sliding for almost seven years. Several factors contributed to the fall of inflation.

The first and most powerful factor was that the Fed lived up to its promise. Money growth slowed and became less volatile, just as had been promised.

Second, by 1980 the public began to accept the possibility that the Fed would be steadfast, and that its announced policy could control inflation.

A third force was the outcome of the presidential election of 1980. For 20 years presidential candidates had argued over which of them could best manage the growing welfare state—and whether it should grow more quickly or more slowly. But in 1980 Ronald Reagan campaigned on a pledge to *reverse* the growth of government. His election appeared to signal that the 1980s would be considerably different from the previous two decades.

The public came to expect reduced inflation, which made people more willing to hold on to money, rather than spend it quickly. So the economy was able to absorb the new money the Fed printed, without an inflationary result.

Economic Expansion

A fourth factor appeared in 1982. The economy began an energetic expansion, which caused incomes and wealth to grow—adding further to the ability to absorb new money without inflation.

The economic expansion was propelled by cuts in income tax rates. The rates were reduced during 1981–83, and then were slashed again in 1987 and 1988. The lower tax rates increased the incentive for people to work, produce, and earn.[3]

The tax-rate cuts held back inflation in another way. Lower taxes made the United States a more attractive place for foreign investors. Capital flowed into the U.S. from all the world. But to invest in the U.S., foreigners first needed to exchange their own currencies for U.S. dollars.

The bidding for U.S. dollars pushed up the foreign exchange value of the dollar. This in turn made foreign products cheaper for Americans.

The inflation rate continued falling—finally reaching bottom, at 1%, at the end of 1986.

[3]The effects of tax-rate reductions are the subject of Chapter 6.

THE END OF THE END OF INFLATION

The Federal Reserve's allegiance to moderation lasted four years.

In late 1982, probably alarmed by the severity of the recession then under way, the Fed fell off the wagon. The rate of money growth shot up to 11% from 7%, and remained close to 10% throughout most of the decade. In 1983, the rate rose to 13% and then swung back to 7% the following year. Monetary stability had been abandoned.

Strong economic growth and confidence in the dollar's ability to hold its value slowed the return of inflation, but the flow of new money guaranteed that inflation *would* return eventually. In 1987, inflation rose from 1% to 4%.

Once again, the Fed abruptly changed course. It slammed on the brakes, and kept the money supply almost unchanged for all of 1987. This violent switch in direction was bound to hurt. The stock market crash of October 1987 was probably the first consequence.

The next consequence probably will be a recession.[4]

Squandered Opportunity

The reformation in Fed policy in 1978, the election mandate of Ronald Reagan in 1980, and the tax cuts of 1981 gave the government an extraordinary opportunity to change the direction and character of the U.S. economy.

Once the recession of 1982 was out of the way, there was a chance to stop the boom-bust, inflation-recession seesaw once and for all. All that was needed was for the Federal Reserve to continue its 1978–82 policy of modest, stable money growth.

But the opportunity was squandered. The Fed gave up and

[4]The stock market crash is discussed further in Chapter 7.

reverted to the stop-and-go policy that had caused so much grief in the 1970s.

The Fed's surrender was a tragedy. In 1982 the economy suffered through its worst recession since the 1930s to get off the inflation-recession seesaw. Now it's back on.

Like the drug addict who breaks the habit and then backslides, the Fed will find it even harder the next time it tries to establish a moderate, credible pattern of money creation. And next time around, the economy's withdrawal symptoms may be much more painful.

THE PRESENT

Intense money growth in 1985 and 1986 was followed by a virtual halt beginning in 1987.

The halt makes a recession in 1989 or 1990 very likely. And, unlike recessions of the past, this one will begin with the economy already in a weak and vulnerable condition.

Given the huge federal deficits and the fragile state of the banking system, there's good reason to expect the recession to be unusually severe.

The Fed has demonstrated that it stands ready to overreact to whatever happens. The first signs of a slowdown should cause the Fed to crank up the printing presses and flood the country with new money. The need for the new money will seem undeniable, and the Fed will be encouraged by the relatively mild inflation of recent years. It will be easy for the Fed to overestimate what it can get away with.

The Fed's efforts won't end the recession immediately. That may take two years or more of new money—long enough to guarantee a fast-forward replay of inflation by 1991.

Here we go again.

3

The Federal Debt Crisis

Politicians, economists, and journalists have been warning us about the federal deficits since the early 1980s.

First there were forecasts of intolerably high interest rates and renewed inflation. But interest rates went down, not up. And, until 1987, inflation remained dormant; even in 1988, at 4%, it was pale stuff compared to the inflation of the 1970s.

Then the deficits were cited as evidence that the prosperity of the decade was phony: we were enjoying ourselves by running up bills that our grandchildren would have to pay.

And we were told that the deficits were being financed by foreign investors; our nation's future was being mortgaged to the whims of foreigners. But, in fact, the percentage of the government's debt held by foreigners has dropped from a high of 18% in 1978 to 12% in 1987.[1]

Although the federal deficits have been a continual worry, none of the dire consequences they seemed to threaten have come to pass.

But, despite the failed predictions, the deficits *are* affecting our

---

[1]*Federal Reserve Bulletin,* (described on page 247 of this book), table 1.41, October 1981 (page A32) and July 1988 (page A30).

future. The problem has been building quietly, and it could erupt within the next few years.

THE DEFICIT & INTEREST RATES

When the federal government spends more than it collects in taxes, it finances the deficit by borrowing. The borrowing is accomplished by selling IOUs to investors. Most of the IOUs—Treasury bonds, Treasury notes, and Treasury bills—are sold to the highest bidders at public auctions.

Large corporations also borrow by selling bonds and other securities at public auction. But the government is different from all other borrowers. Although it won't pay a higher interest rate than it needs to, it can afford to pay whatever rate is necessary. It can't be frozen out of the credit market. If the government must pay 30% to borrow, it will.

Even if no investor bids on the Treasury securities being auctioned, the Federal Reserve will buy them—and pay for the securities with money newly created for the purpose.

Unlike you or me, the government can't be turned down for lack of credit. And for the government, no interest rate is too high.

So the government will always get whatever credit it needs. And the credit it grabs, other potential borrowers—corporations and consumers who can't afford high interest rates—must do without. Thus government borrowing "crowds out" private borrowers. The crowding-out isn't apparent to the victim, who sees only the fact that interest rates are too high, but not the reason for it. And the crowding-out isn't apparent to others because no one keeps records of canceled or would-be borrowing.

Government borrowing increases the demand for credit—putting upward pressure on interest rates. But interest rates don't always rise when the government borrows, because other factors—the availability of credit and the general demand for it—also affect interest rates. At times, interest rates might remain steady, or even fall, while the government's borrowing is increasing.

But government borrowing necessarily makes interest rates higher than they would be if the government weren't borrowing.

The Runaway Train

Because of the constant deficits, there has been a rapid rise in the government's total debt and its need to borrow. At some point, the government's borrowing will be so large that it overwhelms the credit markets and forces interest rates upward—no matter what other borrowers and lenders do.

Because the government refinances about $1 trillion of its debt every year, substantially higher interest rates will substantially increase the government's yearly interest bill. And that will cause the deficit to worsen—which will cause the borrowing to increase—which will push up interest rates—which will increase the government's interest expense—and so on, round and round in a vicious circle. The debt will become a runaway train.

The train leaves the station very slowly. So long as the debt isn't growing faster than the economy itself (so that the ability to pay the debt keeps up with its size), and so long as interest expense isn't more than a small share of the federal budget (so that most of what is spent can still be determined by Congress each year), the train is under control and can still be stopped.

But when growth in the debt outraces growth in the economy, and when interest expense dominates the government's budget, the train will be out of control and accelerate on its own.

Federal debt hasn't yet reached that point, but it's racing toward it. The debt has grown by 182% since 1980, while the economy (as measured by the Gross National Product) has grown by only 76%.[2]

[2]*Economic Indicators* (described on page 247 of this book), July 1988, pages 1 and 32.

In fiscal 1960, 10% of the federal budget went to interest expense. In 1976, the share was still only 10%. But by 1980 it was 13%, and then 16% in 1982, and 19% in 1986.[3]

The growth in interest expense has occurred even though, between 1981 and 1988, the interest rate on Treasury bills fell from 16% to under 7%. When interest rates begin to rise in earnest, interest expense will dominate the budget.

THE DEBT CRISIS

No one can know how soon the government's interest costs will run out of control. But I don't think the time can be very far away.

The government has had everything working in its favor until now. Inflation and interest rates have been declining. And tax receipts have been growing in an expanding economy. But the government's good fortune appears to be running out.

With the debt rising steadily, the government's need for credit grows larger every year. If the next two years bring a recession or inflation—or both—the process will accelerate, and the debt will be out of control. Then the federal debt crisis won't be talk anymore.

Recession

A recession could make the deficit uncontrollable by stretching the budget from both ends. Tax revenues would drop during a recession, because lower incomes yield less in taxes. And government spending would rise, because so many federal programs expand automatically during bad times.

In the 1975 recession, the combination of falling tax revenue

[3]U.S. Department of Commerce, *Statistical Abstract of the United States, 1988,* table 477.

and rising expenditures pushed the deficit up to $53 billion from $5 billion. In the brief 1980 recession, the deficit jumped to $74 billion from $40 billion. In the 1982 recession, the deficit rose to $128 billion from $79 billion.

The next recession will pump up the deficit quickly. The deficit that was $155 billion in 1988 could become $200 or $300 billion or much more during a recession year.

In two years' time, the accumulated federal debt could grow by $500 billion or $600 billion. Even if interest *rates* didn't rise, interest expense that was 19% of the federal budget in 1986 could become 25% of the budget.

But interest rates *would* rise; they always do at the onset of a recession. And with the government floating several hundred billion dollars' worth of new debt every year, interest rates could conceivably go well beyond the 20% prime rate of 1980 and 1981—causing the recession to be much worse than that of 1981–82.

Inflation

Or it might be inflation—such as the inflation resulting from attempts to end the next recession—that pushes the deficit out of control. When the inflation rate rises, so do interest rates. The 15% inflation peak of 1980, for example, sent the rate on Treasury bills up to 16%.

The federal debt today is three times what it was in 1980, so a 16% interest rate could cause the government's annual interest expense to be over 30% of the federal budget. But a 16% rate isn't really the upper limit; the great weight of the federal debt on the credit markets could cause the interest rate on Treasury bills to rise well beyond 16%.

Rising interest rates would be feeding on the debt, the debt feeding on the deficits, the deficits feeding on the interest expense, and the interest expense feeding on rising interest rates. And through it all, the percentage of the federal budget going to interest expense would be getting larger and larger—making it harder for Congress to control federal spending.

Accelerating Inflation

The Federal Reserve might buy a large share of the government's debt—to ease the strain on the credit market and hold down interest rates. For the politicians, this would buy time—time to search for a way out, time to hope that the problem would somehow go away, time to find someone to blame, and (most important) time to get reelected.

But it would soon make matters worse. The Federal Reserve's purchases of Treasury securities would increase the money supply—intensifying inflation.

As inflation grows, interest rates rise—because lenders want to be compensated for the erosion in purchasing power, and because inflation makes it profitable for borrowers to pay the higher rates. The higher interest rates would make the federal deficits worse and require that the Fed print even more new money—causing even more inflation.

And so another vicious circle would begin to spin—one that causes rising deficits and rising inflation to feed on each other. Not too far away, we can see inflation rates that are far beyond the 15% rate that scared us so much in 1980—when the federal debt was only a third of its present size.

WHAT WILL HAPPEN?

To resolve the crisis permanently, the government needs to do more than balance the budget. It must reduce the outstanding debt so that it no longer is such a threat to the economy.

There are only three theoretical possibilities: default on some or all of the debt, raise taxes, or cut spending.

Default

Some people believe the U.S. government will someday default on its debt—either by suspending interest payments, delaying the repayment dates of the principal, or simply declaring all its debts null and void. But I can't imagine any circumstance, no matter how extreme, that would force the government to default on its debt.

By defaulting, the government would cripple itself, since a default would impair its ability to borrow further. And the government always has a ready alternative to defaulting. Even though individuals and corporations sometimes are unable to find the cash to pay their debts, the U.S. government (through the Federal Reserve) can easily print whatever dollars it needs to repay Treasury bills and Treasury bonds in full and on time.

It's important to appreciate the power that comes with owning the license to print U.S. dollars—a license held exclusively by the U.S. government. It is as though you could write checks that everyone would accept but no one would present for payment. That's what the government can do—and has been doing for years—because it doesn't have to back its checks with real resources.

When a Treasury bond matures, the Federal Reserve can, if necessary, create brand-new money to pay off the bond. It's that simple. Congress doesn't have to pass a law to make it possible, no partisan debates precede the act, and it isn't front-page news the next day.

Third-world governments have dishonored their debts, but the situation is wholly different. A third-world government defaults only on debt denominated in foreign currencies, such as the dollar, that it has no ability to print. It doesn't default on IOUs that promise repayment in the country's own currency, because it can print the money to pay those debts.

Over 99% of the U.S. government's debts are denominated in U.S. dollars—and the U.S. government can create U.S. dollars at will. If the government were to default on even a single one of those debts, it would no longer be able to float bonds and bills as it does today.

So the government has no need to default, and it would be foolish to do so.

Income Tax Increase

A more realistic possibility is that income tax rates will be increased. And many people assume that this will be the eventual solution.

Part of the reason for expecting a tax increase is the assumption that the tax-rate cuts of 1981–83 caused the deficits in the first place. But the budget deficit was already $74 billion in 1980.

The tax-rate cuts were the principal force behind the economic expansion that began in 1982. As the tax-cut proponents hoped for in 1981, lower tax rates rejuvenated the economy—bringing larger incomes for the public and greater income-tax revenues for the government.

Government revenues were 76% higher in 1988 than in 1980. The budget deficit persisted because government spending grew just as rapidly as revenues.

Restoring pre-1981 tax rates, or even a maximum rate of 38%, would probably be self-defeating. Such a move would do so much to undo the prosperity of the past six years that it might result in *less* revenue and a bigger deficit.

That doesn't mean the politicians wouldn't like to try it. But, fortunately, the public mood today is very cool toward higher income tax rates.[4]

[4]The way income tax rates affect the economy is discussed further in Chapter 6.

Other Taxes

So there may be political pressure for new taxes of other kinds—such as higher excise taxes or a new value-added tax (VAT).

It's true that non-income taxes inhibit investment and productivity less than income taxes do, but any kind of tax is a drag on the economy. No matter how the government raises money, government expenditures take resources (goods, services, manpower, and the like) away from productive individuals. Whatever the government controls or consumes will leave the private economy that much poorer.

It isn't likely that any form of tax increase could produce enough revenue to close the deficit without at the same time throwing the economy into a tailspin. And the tailspin would lead to *lower* tax revenues. We'd be stuck with higher taxes, a depressed economy, and a deficit at least as large as we have now.

And there's no assurance that any new revenue would even be applied to reduce the deficit. It might be used instead to accommodate requests for money that the government has up to now turned down.

Until now, the deficits have at least served the purpose of discouraging new spending programs. Federal spending increased by only 5% in 1986, 1% in 1987, and 5% in 1988—down from a yearly average of 10% for the prior five years.[5]

Spending Cuts

The only approach that's certain to cut the deficit is to reduce government spending.

Tax revenues have continued to rise because of a prosperous economy. An absolute spending freeze for only about 2½ years would allow yearly tax revenues to catch up with expenditures. Or

[5]*Economic Indicators* (described on page 247), May 1988, page 32.

spending could continue to grow at the slow rates of the last 3 years, and the budget could be balanced within 3 to 4 years.

WHAT ARE OUR CHANCES?

Because interest expense hasn't yet taken over the federal budget, there's still time to avoid a debt crisis—but only if the government makes deep cuts in spending before the next severe recession and before the next round of inflation.

More likely, the government will tinker with the problem by enacting a tax increase—one that appears to cut the deficit somewhat, but doesn't make too many people upset. At the same time, there may be cosmetic spending cuts that turn out later to have been illusory.

Meanwhile, as discussed in Chapter 2, the Federal Reserve's tight-money policy of 1987 and 1988 has aimed us at a recession that could begin in 1989 or 1990. The arrival of the recession would be the trigger that transforms the debt crisis from small talk to big trouble.

The debt crisis won't destroy the economy, but it could cripple it. Interest rates could soar to levels we've never seen before—creating mass unemployment and mass bankruptcies.

Even then, the government probably would continue to fiddle with the problem—employing combinations of tax increases and insignificant spending cuts that continually promise relief but, in fact, do little. The economic stagnation could continue for years—or even decades.

Eventually, there will have to be massive spending cuts, since that's the only way out of the debt problem. If the cuts come soon, the entire crisis may be avoided; if they come later, we will all suffer first.

What are the chances for an immediate solution? You can answer that question by asking who it is that takes the problem seriously enough to do something about it.

You heard President Bush's campaign speeches. Which programs did he promise to cut? Which interest groups were told that they couldn't have what they want right now?

And Congress up to now has treated the slightest dip in the deficit as an opportunity to push new spending programs. It is one thing to agree on the need for budget reduction; it is something else to get 535 drunken sailors onto the same boat at the same time.

4

The Banking Crisis

A banking crisis would touch you much more directly than the other crises. If the automated teller you visit on Saturdays says "Empty," or if your checks bounce because your *bank* has insufficient funds, you won't need to read a newspaper to find out that something is terribly wrong.

The failure rate for commercial banks has been growing since 1981, when only 10 banks were closed. There were 42 failures in 1982, 48 in 1983, 79 in 1984, 120 in 1985, and 138 in 1986. And 184 banks failed in 1987—the worst year for bank failures since the Great Depression. Over the same period, 205 savings & loan associations either failed or had to be saved by the government.

Still, the problem may not have worried you. The banks and savings & loans you read about are only a tiny fraction of all financial institutions. And they seem to be special cases—banks in areas dependent on the oil industry (hurt by the recent collapse in oil prices) and banks that have made foolish loans.

And, no matter what happens, you know that your bank deposit is insured by an agency of the federal government. You're counting on the U.S. government to do whatever is necessary to assure the safety of your deposit—by propping up your bank in hard

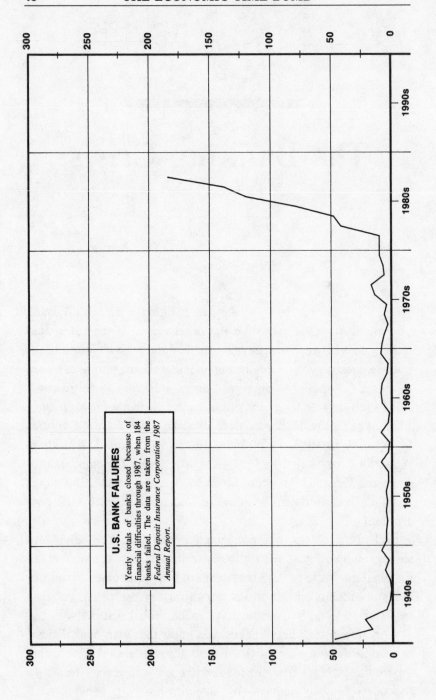

U.S. BANK FAILURES

Yearly totals of banks closed because of financial difficulties through 1987, when 184 banks failed. The data are taken from the *Federal Deposit Insurance Corporation 1987 Annual Report.*

times, and by keeping the FDIC and FSLIC deposit insurance programs solvent.[1]

Unfortunately, these comforting thoughts may be dangerously wrong. The banking system has problems that go much deeper than its loans to oil producers and shaky third-world governments. The underlying weakness won't be fixed by replacing the paltry billions that banks have lost in Texas and Brazil.

For you to survive the economic time bomb, your plans should allow for these possibilities:

- Almost all banks and savings & loan associations will be in trouble.
- Their problems will overwhelm the deposit insurance funds.
- Congress will stall when asked to back up the deposit insurance system.
- The banking problems will aggravate the monetary and budget crises.

To understand why you need to take these possibilities seriously, we need to look at the way U.S. banks operate.[2]

OPERATION OF A BANK

A bank earns its living by taking in money from depositors, and lending the money to its customers or investing it. The bank's gross profit is the difference between the interest it earns and the interest it pays.

A bank's assets are its cash holdings, its outstanding loans (the money owed to it by borrowers), and its investments. Its main

[1]The Federal Deposit Insurance Corporation (FDIC) and the Federal Savings & Loan Insurance Corporation (FSLIC) are the government agencies that insure bank deposits and savings & loan deposits, respectively.
[2]On page 57, I'll discuss the difference between banks and savings & loan associations. Otherwise, all references to banks apply to savings & loans and credit unions as well.

liabilities are its outstanding deposits—money it owes to its depositors.

Because a bank generally can earn a greater return on loans than on investments, it will lend out as much of its money as it dares. A bank may tie up nearly all of its assets in loans—if it's confident that only a few of its depositors will want to withdraw their money on any day or in any short period.

A bank fails when it doesn't have enough cash available to pay the depositors who want to withdraw their money—even if the bank's assets are worth enough money to pay everyone eventually.

Matching Maturities

For a bank, *liquidity* is the key—the availability of enough cash (or assets that can be converted to cash immediately) to honor all withdrawal requests.

To be liquid, a bank doesn't need to leave all its money sitting in the vault. But it does need to arrange its loans and investments to allow for the promises the bank has made to its depositors.

For example, checking account deposits are repayable to the depositor on demand. A bank can use these deposits to buy U.S. Treasury bills or other short-term, interest-bearing securities for itself—knowing that those investments can be converted to cash virtually at a moment's notice.

Or it can use that money to make margin loans on stocks and bonds. The bank retains the right to demand repayment of those loans at any time, and to sell the securities on the spot to enforce repayment.

In these cases, a bank earns interest on the money that has been deposited with it, but it still is able to return the money to depositors whenever requested.

A bank also can make loans that won't be repaid for months or years, and still remain liquid. To do so, it needs to match those loans to time deposits or CDs (certificates of deposit) that run for similar periods. For example, it can make 3-year auto loans using money raised through 3-year CDs. The loan will be repaid by the time the depositor must be repaid.

If a bank wants to make 20-year or 30-year mortgages at fixed interest rates, it needs to finance them with long-term CDs or bonds.

Since term loans normally are repaid in monthly payments, rather than in a single payment at the end of the term, not all the money for a 3-year loan has to come from a 3-year deposit. But the repayment schedules of the bank's loans, taken as a whole, should match the terms of the deposits that the bank has received. Otherwise, the bank isn't fully liquid.

In Practice

The virtue of "matching maturities"—matching 1-year loans to 1-year deposits, and so on—is a lesson taught in basic college finance classes. And it is simple common sense.

But, unfortunately, American banks don't do business that way. In practice, banks routinely use money repayable to depositors on demand to finance 1-year loans or, worse yet, 30-year mortgages.

A banker mismatches maturities deliberately to increase his profit margin. He'd much rather earn 11% on a mortgage than 7% on Treasury bills.

But a bank with mismatched maturities is an illiquid bank. It never has the liquid assets to satisfy all the depositors who could demand payment. The bank is vulnerable to any event that might lead to greater-than-expected withdrawals.

And yet bankers sleep well at night, without dreams of angry depositors demanding their money.

GOVERNMENT PROTECTION OF BANKS

If a banker were afraid of sudden, heavy deposit withdrawals, he wouldn't mismatch maturities. He would fear that someday some event—a stock market crash, civil disorder, troubles at other banks, or some other financial crisis—would trigger a rush of withdrawals by anxious depositors.

But the government has relieved banks of this worry by reassuring depositors that their money will always be there when they want it.

Reassuring depositors isn't easy. Federal and state governments have regulated banks, for the supposed safety of depositors, in one way or another since the founding of the republic. Since 1913, the Federal Reserve System has been one tool of reassurance—since the Fed possesses seemingly unlimited power to lend money to illiquid banks. But depositors in the 1930s didn't get the message; runs against banks were widespread, and 4,004 banks failed in 1933 alone.[3]

Stickers

So, in 1934, the government began giving stickers to banks to place in their windows. The stickers said that every deposit in the bank was insured up to $2,500 by an agency of the United States government. (Over the years, the coverage has been increased to $100,000.)

The message on the sticker is impressive, even if the resources behind it aren't.

The Federal Deposit Insurance Corporation (FDIC) is the government agency that operates the deposit insurance program. It has a reserve fund, financed by insurance premiums paid by all

[3]*Historical Statistics of the United States, Colonial Times to 1970* (U.S. Department of Commerce), page 2038, series X741.

commercial banks, to pay off depositors when a bank fails. The reserve fund currently equals about 1% of the deposits it is meant to cover.[4]

Like any insurer, the FDIC can handle an isolated disaster—the deposits lost in a bank that, all by itself, goes under. And up to now, the FDIC has managed to clean up every bank failure promptly.

But the FDIC couldn't hope to cover a nationwide banking crisis of the kind that overwhelmed banks in the 1930s. Such a crisis is an uninsurable risk. No insurance system could possibly cover it, just as no auto insurance company could cover a nationwide car pileup.

The FDIC's function isn't to reimburse you in the event of a nationwide banking crisis, or to protect you from weak banks. The FDIC's job is to stop you from withdrawing your money when you get worried.

The FDIC assumes that bank crises occur because depositors are overly anxious about their money—not because banks mismanage the money. The FDIC's strategy is to *avoid* the kinds of bank runs that occurred in the 1930s, not to pay you if they happen—although by promising to do the second, it hopes to accomplish the first.

RISKY BUSINESS

Reassured by FDIC insurance, depositors seldom consider a bank's financial condition. One bank is as safe as another if you're depending on the U.S. government, rather than the bank's management, for safety.

Thus FDIC insurance removes the restraining influence that depositors otherwise would exert on bank management. A cau-

[4]Federal Deposit Insurance Corporation, *1987 Annual Report,* page 63.

tious bank policy ceases to be a tool with which to attract new deposits.

With depositors no longer watching over banks, the federal government has been forced to regulate banks very tightly—limiting the interest rates that banks could pay to depositors, restricting the types of investments a bank could hold and the kinds of business it could enter, and deciding who could own or manage a bank.

But all the inspectors from the Comptroller of the Currency, the Federal Reserve System, the Federal Home Loan Banks, the FDIC, the FSLIC, and state regulatory agencies failed to discover and head off the problems that caused 521 banks and 141 savings & loans to go under during 1984–87.[5]

Operating under the cover of an FDIC sticker, a bank needn't worry that its lending practices will scare off depositors. It's free to take any risk that government regulations don't forbid.

So banks deliberately forsake liquidity by mismatching maturities, in order to obtain the higher interest rates available on long-term loans.

Making Decisions

Despite the FDIC sticker in his window, a banker still has an incentive to act prudently; if his bank is ruined by risky loans, the FDIC will bail out his depositors, but it won't bail him out.

Like any other businessman, a banker probably will weigh risks carefully. No regulator has to tell him to be prudent. (If a regulator had a better eye for risk than the banker, the banker probably would try to hire him.)

It's when a bank is in trouble that the sticker becomes dangerous. When a string of loans has gone bad, or reserves have become dangerously small, or rising interest rates have

---

[5]FDIC *1987 Annual Report,* page 49, and information given to the author by the Federal Home Loan Bank Board.

squeezed profits, then a banker may decide that his best chance of recovering is to gamble. With one big score, he might be able to recoup everything.

And because of the FDIC sticker, no depositors are looking over the banker's shoulder when he decides to bet the bank.

The most likely avenue for gambling is with a few, big, risky loans that pay exceptionally high rates of interest. A well-secured mortgage, for example, might earn 10%, but a construction loan might return 14%. Or if the contractor is in shaky financial condition, or the local real-estate market is weak, the loan might pay 16%.

Third-World Loans

Understanding the regulatory cocoon in which banks have operated helps us to see how some bankers could have thought that loans to third-world governments were as sound as buying U.S. Treasury securities, and how other bankers could think they were safe when all their loans were tied to one industry—such as oil.

For years, bankers didn't have to think like businessmen. They were part of a government-sponsored cartel. They didn't have to provide convenient hours of service for their customers, they didn't have to demonstrate prudence to their depositors, they didn't have to worry that competitors would offer higher interest rates or better service. In short, they were bureaucrats, not entrepreneurs.

Making loans to third-world governments wasn't a mistake. After all, someone was going to do it. But making loans at interest rates reserved for the safest borrowers, and lending so much that a bank's solvency became dependent on one borrower's timely repayment—these were mistakes that no real-world businessman would make.

The cloistered environment created by deposit insurance has

fostered a race of bankers who don't look at their customers, their business, and their risks in the way that normal business-men do.

INTEREST RATES & PROFITS

A bank chooses to mismatch maturities because short-term deposits are cheaper to attract than long-term deposits, and because long-term loans earn more than short-term loans.

An earnings-conscious banker would rather pay 6% on a 1-year CD than 8% on a 5-year CD. And he'd rather lend the money on a 30-year mortgage earning 11% than on a 5-year loan earning 10%. With a 30-year loan financed out of short-term deposits, he has a gross profit of 5%. With a 5-year loan financed out of 5-year CDs, he has a gross profit of only 2%.

Mismatching maturities can work nicely for a bank so long as interest rates are stable. But if interest rates rise, the bank may have to pay 8% to get the depositor to renew his CD when it comes due at the end of the year—even though the bank will continue to receive only 11% on the mortgage. Its gross profit margin declines from 5% to 3%.

If interest rates continue rising, the bank may have to pay *more* than 11% to hold on to deposits. Then it will lose money on every 11% loan still on the books.

That's what happened in 1981. The tide of rising interest rates forced banks to pay 15% or more on CDs, while they still earned only 6% to 11% on old mortgages.

Banks are hurt when rising interest rates turn existing long-term loans into losers. The collapse of inflation in the early 1980s rescued many banks by reversing a 30-year upward trend in inter-est rates. However, for many others, it only prolonged the agony. Slowly but surely their problems are coming to light—and every year a larger number of banks go under.

During the next inflation, interest rates will rise sharply. With so many banks now crowding the edge of bankruptcy, it's likely that large numbers of them will tumble over that edge.

BANKS VS. SAVINGS & LOANS

Banks, savings & loans, and credit unions all mismatch maturities.

But savings & loans are the worst offenders. Their portfolios are dominated by long-term mortgages, yet they try no harder than banks to attract long-term deposits. So it isn't surprising that the banking crisis hit the savings & loans first.

The situation may have deteriorated further by the time you read this. But as of June 30, 1988, the reserve fund of the Federal Savings & Loan Insurance Corporation had already shrunk to $2.5 billion—which was only 0.3% of the $967 billion in deposits it was supposed to be protecting.

The FSLIC had already judged 511 savings & loans to be insolvent. But it couldn't afford to close them, because the cost of paying off depositors would have been $30.9 billion—$28.4 billion more than the FSLIC's entire reserve fund.[6]

THE EMERGING CRISIS

The Federal Deposit Insurance Corporation is headed for a similar crisis. As of December 31, 1987, the FDIC had a reserve fund of $18.3 billion to protect insured deposits of $1,659 billion—coverage of only 1.1%.[7]

The banking crisis is still localized and manageable. But the banks are vulnerable to any event that worries depositors, increases loan defaults, or causes interest rates to rise. The banking

[6]Information given to the author by the Federal Home Loan Bank Board.
[7]FDIC *1987 Annual Report,* page 63.

system has survived the past six years only because the economy has managed to avoid the shock of either a recession or severe inflation.

A severe recession could cause banks everywhere to suffer loan losses on the scale that has afflicted banks in the oil-producing states. Increased inflation would drive up interest rates and turn a bank's fixed-rate loans and mortgages into money losers. For many banks, the losses would wipe out any capital they hadn't left in Brazil.

Up to now, the FDIC has been able to close or merge every failing bank and repay its depositors promptly and in full. But the failing banks have all been relatively small. Now both the number and size of FDIC bail-outs are expanding.

And the FDIC's resources will be shrinking. Since 1935, the FDIC's income from premiums has always exceeded its outlays. The annual surplus was larger year after year until 1983—when FDIC income exceeded outlays by $1.658 billion. But since then the annual surplus has been shrinking—falling to only $49 million in 1987, the lowest level since 1941.[8]

The next banking scandal may involve a major bank—one that would eat up a large fraction of the FDIC's $18-billion reserve fund. And more than one such scandal would impair confidence in the FDIC itself—possibly leading many depositors to decide to withdraw their money from the banking system in fear of losing their savings.

This is known as a run on the bank. Because mismatching maturities is the norm, very few banks could withstand a run.

GOVERNMENT TO THE RESCUE

Of course, the government would try to head off any banking crisis.

For a while, the Federal Reserve System would continue to lend

[8]FDIC *1987 Annual Report,* page 62.

money to illiquid banks. The FDIC would pay off depositors at banks that failed. And if the FDIC ran out of money, Congress would be called upon to appropriate funds from the government's general budget.

But both the Fed and Congress would be overwhelmed by the crisis.

Federal Reserve Help

The Federal Reserve System may stand ready to lend money to any bank that gets into trouble. But I think it would be foolish to assume that no important bank will ever fail. The Fed knows that its assistance has a cost to the economy, so the assistance can't be unlimited.

When the Fed lends money to a bank, it creates the money out of thin air—just as it does when buying the government's bonds. And new money, whatever it is used for, feeds inflation.

When a banking crisis erupts in earnest, the Fed may intend to save every major bank. But eventually it will be obvious that the price will be inflation of 15%, 25%, or worse. At some point, the chaos of a banking collapse might be judged to be a smaller catastrophe to endure than a Nicaraguan-style inflation.

Commercial banks and savings & loans owe roughly $3.2 *trillion* to their depositors. If the Federal Reserve had to provide even 5% of that amount, it would increase the nation's money supply by 57%—perhaps within the space of a few months. The American economy has never experienced an inflationary shock so violent—not even during wartime. I doubt that the Fed would risk it.[9]

And if it did, you and I would have to cope with runaway inflation. The prices of nearly everything we buy would be rising daily. And the banks would have to cope with trouble much worse than that which prompted the Fed's original bail-out.

---

[9]The money supply increase was determined by calculating the effect of the Fed's injections on the monetary base. Source of data: *U.S. Financial Data,* Federal Reserve Bank of St. Louis, August 18, 1988, page 2.

We can't know in advance what the governors of the Federal Reserve System will consider to be a tolerable level of inflation or a tolerable level of bank failures. Your investment program is too risky if it relies on anyone's estimate of how much help the Federal Reserve will give the banking industry.

Congress to the Rescue

Because the Federal Reserve won't be able to stop a bank panic, the FDIC and the FSLIC will eventually run out of money—perhaps on the first day of a run on banks. And Congress will be asked to appropriate the money needed to pay off depositors.

But with the federal budget over $150 billion per year out of balance now, and with the government's interest expense already threatening to accelerate beyond control, Congress is in no position to provide a blank check to anyone.

Whatever Congress does will pump up the federal deficit. If the new debt is financed by selling bonds to the public, interest rates will rocket to the moon (making the banking crisis worse). If the new debt is financed by selling bonds to the Federal Reserve, inflation and interest rates both will rocket to the moon (also making the banking crisis worse).

That doesn't mean Congress won't act, but the government's own runaway debt problem—plus the realities of politics—will keep the response of Congress from being as swift and sure and complete as bank depositors will be wishing for.

Panic in the Pork Barrel

Suppose, for example, that the banking crisis is triggered by a recession, when loan defaults are driving banks to the wall. Because of the recession, federal spending will be up and tax revenues down.

The FDIC won't be the only one asking for money. There will be pleas for aid from other federal agencies, from state and local governments, and from large companies employing hundreds of thousands of voters.

Congress won't be able to satisfy 100% of every demand made of it. So it will allocate the available money through the great game of politics—complete with compromises, back-scratching, face-saving, press releases, and the survival of the fittest congressman. The process will be similar to hammering out a pork-barrel public works bill.

There will be intense disagreements within Congress, and between Congress and the president, over the cause of the crisis and what should be done to end it. Some congressmen will resist a bail-out in order to gain concessions on other issues. And many of them will be more interested in fixing the blame than in fixing the problem. The disagreements might delay relief for the FDIC for months—and almost certainly would turn the relief into something other than simple, full payment for depositors.

Most likely, Congress would meet some, but not all, of the FDIC's commitments. It might pay off all claims at 50 cents on the dollar—perhaps promising to cover the rest later. Or you might get everything, but only after waiting several months for the FDIC to catch up on its paperwork—and watching runaway inflation chew up the value of the bank deposit you can't touch.

Or Congress might cover the FDIC's commitments on deposits only up to, say, $25,000—justifying the policy as the best deal possible for the "little guy," who needs help the most.[10]

The president might even declare a bank holiday—a period in which all banks are closed by government decree—while Congress, the FDIC, and other regulators sort out the problems (even though a bank holiday is the very event the FDIC was created to prevent).

---

[10]Of course, this might hurt the "little guy" who invested $10,000 in a money market fund that bought $1-million CDs from banks that went broke.

Through it all, the government would deny that it was letting the FDIC fail. However many promises were broken, the overriding theme would be that the integrity of deposit insurance is being preserved—just as Hitler, Stalin, and Brezhnev preserved the integrity of Czechoslovakia.

Precisely what path Congress would take is unforeseeable. All we know is that FDIC insurance would be a political football, just as Social Security has become.

Like Social Security, FDIC insurance gives you the absolute right to receive whatever Congress decides to give you.

Escape from the Maze

No matter what the FDIC does, no matter what Congress or the Federal Reserve does, once the banking crisis hits full stride, there will be no chance for a happy ending. Bank deposits will be lost, or interest rates will shoot above 1980's 20% rates, or inflation will break out well beyond its last peak of 15%.

And it's very possible that we'll see all these things.

CONSEQUENCES

If there is a nationwide banking crisis, it will affect more than just your own bank account.

A banking crisis touches almost everything—including the bank accounts of your employer and the companies in which you've invested. A crisis might prevent your employer from paying your salary, or make it impossible for others to pay you what they owe you.

Most money market funds will be hurt. Because they *do* match maturities precisely, money market funds are perfectly liquid. But most funds invest heavily in CDs issued by banks that aren't liquid. If those banks go under, the redemption value of the money fund shares will be reduced.

Timing

No one can foretell when such a crisis will erupt and overwhelm the FDIC. If an event were predictable, we wouldn't call it a "crisis."

But the number of bank failures and their costs have been rising rapidly throughout the 1980s. And bank problems aren't isolated from other economic problems. Banks would be squeezed tighter and tighter by rising interest rates—whether caused by an uncontrolled federal deficit or by rising inflation. When either of those problems explodes, it could take your bank with it.

Fortunately, you don't have to read the future to be safe. In Part II, I'll explain an investment plan that allows you to be ready for the worst possibilities—even as you profit from however much prosperity remains.

5

Dangerous
Non-Problems

When a government program causes trouble, the government doesn't stop the program; it starts another one.

The new program may ease the pain caused by the first one, but it probably will cause further trouble of its own—leading to yet another call for the government to do something. This is why government tends to grow and grow, amid the debris of half-solved problems.

In the 1960s, for example, the government sought to protect consumers by imposing price controls on natural gas. Not surprisingly, this discouraged the development of new gas wells (and also of new oil wells), thereby increasing American dependence on imported oil. When OPEC struck in 1973, our own government had already made us vulnerable.

Rather than abolish the price controls on natural gas, the government *extended* them to oil. It also imposed rationing and other measures to reduce consumption of petroleum products.

One of those measures was a set of mandatory fuel-efficiency standards for the automobile industry. The standards were easily satisfied by foreign manufacturers, who were already producing cars with small engines, but they required expensive retooling by the American auto industry. The Chrysler Corporation, the weakest of U.S. carmakers, was pushed to the edge of bankruptcy.

But rather than repeal the price controls on oil and gas, or end rationing, or drop the fuel-efficiency requirements, the government established yet another program—a loan guarantee for Chrysler.

Acts & Consequences

The size and absurdity of the Chrysler case make it easy to show how each event led to the next. But it isn't so easy to trace the harm done by thousands of smaller burdens the government places on the economy.

The government has very little productive power of its own. It can pay for its programs only by taking from the economy. The money and services the government gives away are paid for in three ways: (1) by taxing—which hurts all economic activity; (2) by borrowing—which pushes interest rates upward and reduces the credit available to other borrowers; or (3) by printing the money—which fuels inflation and disrupts everyone's plans.

Months, or even years, can separate the government's actions from their unintended consequences. The delay allows the government to escape blame, and gives it time to point an accusing finger elsewhere. The confusion might even make it seem that only the government can solve the new problem.

If government price controls lead to a gasoline shortage, the government can blame the oil companies, impose windfall-profits taxes on oil producers, and ration gasoline.

If the government causes inflation by printing too much paper money, it can blame businessmen for charging too much, workers for wanting too much, and consumers for spending too much—

blame anyone but the government itself. Then the government will happily respond to pleas for wage and price controls as the only apparent way to defeat inflation.

If the government's regulation of banks encourages risky lending practices, the ensuing bank failures will be evidence that banks need *more* regulating.

And even though the growth of government spending outruns inflation, the Gross National Product, population growth, and every other imaginable yardstick, we're still told that the federal deficit is evidence that the government suffers from a shortage of revenue.

BUILDING TO A CLIMAX

Heaping more government on top of government-made problems is a practice as old as government itself. It's easy to feel that, somehow, the economy can always accommodate one more government program—like cramming one more passenger into a bus or stuffing one more sock into a suitcase.

But the 1970s showed what happens eventually when the problems are piled too high: the oil crisis, 15% inflation, wage and price controls, and recessions of greater and greater severity.

There *is* a limit for the bus, the suitcase, and the economy.

No Way Out

We've reached the point where the government can no longer relieve any one of the three big problems—the erratic monetary policy, the dangerously large federal deficits, and the weak banking system—without intensifying another one almost immediately.

If the government attempts to return to the moderate, noninflationary monetary policy of 1978–82, it probably will bring on a severe recession. That would increase loan defaults and would weaken the banking system further. And a recession would cut tax revenues drastically—making the budget deficits that much worse.

If the government tries to save the banks by pouring money into the deposit insurance fund, that too will worsen the deficits. If it tries to rescue banks with massive loans from the Federal Reserve, the new money will bring on acute inflation.

If the government attempts to reduce the budget deficits by increasing tax rates, it will undo the prosperity of the 1980s, probably bring on a painful recession—or worse—and push more banks over the edge. If it tries to get us out of the recession by printing more money, the ensuing inflation and rising interest rates will send another wave of banks over the edge.

Each of the three major problems is itself a ticking time bomb. And anything done to slow one down will speed up the others.

TIMING

I find it hard to imagine that any of these problems can remain dormant much longer. There's evidence that each of them is becoming harder to manage.

Federal borrowing now dominates the credit markets, with bond prices reacting nervously whenever the government announces new deficit figures. And the bank problems and the weakness of the Federal Deposit Insurance Corporation have already reached public view; if the public loses confidence in the FDIC, a massive run on banks will be under way. And the tight money of 1987 and 1988 has probably set the stage for a recession in 1989 or 1990.

But no matter how certain we may feel about the economy's problems, no one can forecast the pace of events. By its nature, a crisis contains an element of surprise. How it will unfold is simply unknowable.

Shocks & Non-Problems

The problems are well enough advanced, however, that a single shock could turn any one of them into a crisis. The other two would soon follow.

Such a shock might be a government attempt to fix some small problem of its own making. Or the shock might come from a new government effort to fix something that isn't broken—an attempt to solve a non-problem. A non-problem is an issue that's been exploited by politicians or the press as an excuse for more government. Non-problems aren't harmful to the economy; some are even symptoms of economic strength.

Non-problems are such things as the trade deficit, the stock market crash, and America's apparent new status as a debtor nation. The list is never complete; almost every day, it seems, someone thinks of a grave new problem we must hurry to remedy.

Two themes usually accompany the handwringing: (1) the people in general, or some villainous element, have failed to handle their affairs responsibly; and (2) only the government can make things right.

GOVERNMENT TO THE RESCUE

Since most people would be hard pressed to name a single problem the government has ever solved once and for all, it's surprising that anyone would think that we need more government.

When someone suggests that only government can handle a problem, I wonder if he's ever tried to mail a package at a government post office or stood in line waiting to get a driver's license or a passport from a government bureau.

Sixty years after the advent of farm subsidies—sixty years of larger and larger subsidies—we continue to hear about hard times on the farm. Fifty years after Social Security was established to ease the financial uncertainties of old age, elderly people wait insecurely each year to see how Congress will change the system.

But no matter how many examples of government failure I might cite, you can be sure that the next big problem to arise will come wrapped in a plea for the government to solve it.

The Heavier Load

Each new government solution further burdens the economy.

The additional load can seem small enough: a few more regulations that business must obey, some more taxes your employer must collect for the government, a few more papers to be filled out every month, another little bite out of your income, another product priced out of the market—or pushed out.

But every new intrusion leaves the economy weaker, and the problem that inspired the intrusion is never solved.

You may not be aware that the government has easy access to your personal banking history and other financial records as a result of the Bank Secrecy Act—which was passed in 1970 as part of the War on Drugs. The act increased the cost of bank services considerably, and now you can keep your financial affairs private only through elaborate efforts to tiptoe around the law. Yet drugs today are more plentiful, more widely consumed, and a bigger scandal than they were in 1970.

When government passes punitive new laws to fight drugs, discrimination, tax evasion, or anything else, we're assured that the innocent have nothing to fear. "If you're doing nothing wrong [or if you have nothing to hide], why should you object to the law?"

But it's the innocent who get trampled in the rush to catch criminals—while the criminals, being full-time professionals, escape the burden of the law. The innocent must endure the indignity of letting government employees search through one's private affairs for evidence of drug dealing or tax evasion.

Businessmen who are innocent are still sentenced to filling out dozens of forms, dealing with nosy bureaucrats, and appearing before tribunals to prove that they didn't discriminate against someone.

The costs of "doing nothing wrong" or "having nothing to hide" can be enormous. And these costs affect all of us. They add to the prices we pay for products, make it more difficult for employers and employees to come to terms, make it harder to obtain insurance, and add uncertainty to everyone's life.

And by weakening the economy, each of them lowers the threshold at which the economy's real problems will turn into full-blown crises.

THE FINAL SHOCK

How close are we to detonating the time bomb?

No one can know precisely. But when our real problems spill over the threshold, it won't be obvious that the government's last little program made the difference. Instead, something else will be blamed—no doubt something the government will volunteer to fix.

The economic time bomb could go off because the public loses faith in the FDIC and causes a general run on the banks, or because a recession makes the federal deficit literally unmanageable. But it also could be the government's next crusade to solve a non-problem that finally detonates the bomb.

The next four chapters will explore the non-problems that have received the most attention recently—including the government's supposed need for more revenue, the stock market crash, the trade deficit, and the idea that America is now a debtor nation.

Each of them calls for the government to do something. Each solution would be, at best, another burden for the economy to bear—lowering the threshold of crisis a little more. At worst, the solution could be the shock that causes the time bomb to explode.

6

Tax Rates
& the Economy

The journalists, economists, and politicians who opposed the tax cuts of 1981–83 now blame the cuts for the large federal deficits. In the spirit of "I told you so," they insist that the new president will be forced to raise taxes sooner or later—that there simply is no other way to pull the government out of the red.

Few of us would welcome paying higher taxes. So if a tax hike is proposed, it probably will be labelled a "temporary surtax" or an attempt "to make the rich pay their fair share," or a special tax dedicated to paying down the national debt.

But, no matter what the politicians might call a tax increase, they would be playing with dynamite. Any increase in taxes would speed up the clock on the economic time bomb. A big enough increase would set it off.

Taxes are a brake on all productive activity, and the economy is highly sensitive to how tightly the brake is set. The higher the tax rates, the greater the drag on the economy.

Tax-rate cuts transformed the crises of the 1970s into the prosperity of the 1980s. The cuts have been the single most constructive economic force of the past decade. Reversing them could be the single most destructive force of the coming decade.

TAX RATES & PROSPERITY

The 1980s began with a maximum tax rate on personal income of 70%, and are ending with a maximum rate of only 28%.[1]

This sharp reduction in tax rates had a powerful effect on the economy, allowing it to grow more rapidly. Lower tax rates encouraged productivity by letting productive people keep more of what they produce.

Motivation

Some people will work hard even when there's no reward. Others will remain idle no matter what they're offered.

But most individuals are affected, to a greater or lesser degree, by the size of the reward they expect. The larger the take-home pay (or return on an investment), the more they will work (or invest).

The tax cuts of the 1980s increased the motivation for productive activity many times over. The tax collector didn't go away, but he had to settle for less.

With lower tax rates, entrepreneurs and workers could keep more of what they earned, and so they worked harder. Investment money flowed from tax shelters and other nonproductive areas into stocks, new companies, and the expansion of existing companies.

[1]The current tax code applies an effective rate of 33% on the taxable income falling between $71,900 and $171,090 (for joint returns). But any income above $171,090 is taxed at only 28%.

The results were new jobs, a greater supply of goods and services, and a more prosperous country.

Incentives

Suppose, for example, that an employed individual is offered the chance to work an extra 10 hours. After considering the other ways he could spend his time, he might decide that he's willing to accept the extra work if it would put an additional $200 in his pocket. If the extra work is worth, say, $260 to his employer, both parties can benefit from getting it done—unless taxes get in the way.

At a tax rate of 30%, the employee would net only $182 (after taxes) for doing a job costing his employer $260. So the worker probably will decline the offer.

But at a tax rate of 20%, the employee would take home $208 from the employer's payment of $260. So the work will be done— and the employee, the employer, and the economy will all be better off.

The tax collector will be better off as well, because a 20% rate brings him $52 in tax, while a 30% rate brings him nothing.

Investments

In the same way, an investor might be willing to risk his money on a new business project for a potential return of at least 10% per year. So the chance to earn a 13% return would seem attractive—were it not for the tax collector.

After paying tax at a rate of 30%, the 13% return leaves the investor with only 9.1%. So the investor will pass up the opportunity, the project will die, and no new jobs will be created.

Instead, the investor will spend his money on a bigger house or on some other form of personal consumption—which gives the economy a small immediate stimulus, but no lasting benefit.

Or he'll invest his money in gold or collectibles or something else that produces no current income—and thus incurs no immediate taxes at all. Or he'll invest the money in a tax shelter. Or perhaps he'll invest it outside the country without informing the tax collector. In any of these cases, his actions add little or nothing to the economy.

But at a tax rate of 20%, the business project offering a 13% return would be practical, since the investor would net 10.4% after taxes. And so the investment would be made—with lasting benefit to the investor himself, to workers, and to the economy.

The tax collector would be better off, too, since a 20% tax on the investor's profits produces more revenue than a 30% tax on nothing.

The Rich and the Would-Be Rich

Any cut made in any tax bracket helps the economy. But the biggest benefit comes from reductions in the *maximum* tax rate, since the health of the economy is affected most by the people with the most money to invest and the most talent and effort to give.

They are the ones who make new enterprises succeed with their capital, their skills, and their ambition. And they are the ones who feel the maximum tax rate most acutely—either because they have high incomes or are striving for them.

If the maximum tax rate is too high, the wealthy investor will put his money into tax shelters, nonproductive assets, or something else that avoids taxes and provides little benefit to the economy. And the talented entrepreneur might choose to earn no more than a decent living—spending more of his time and talent outside his career, content with non-financial satisfactions.

Permanent reductions in the maximum tax rates unleash the wealth of the rich, the energy of the talented, and the hustle of millions who crave the rewards of hard work. The result is more wealth for everyone—flowing from new companies and services, and from more and better jobs.

Because the top rate is so critical, even the 1981 reduction in the maximum rate from 70% to 50% had an impact on the economy. It increased the take-home portion of investment income to 50% from 30%—making an investor's return over half again as large.

Effect on Inflation

The tax cuts also helped to reduce inflation.

First, they helped the economy expand, which made people wealthier—increasing the amount of cash they wanted to hold, rather than spend quickly. This greater demand to hold money reduced the inflationary effect that usually results from the printing of new money.

Second, lower tax rates made the United States a more attractive place for foreign investors—since the U.S. government taxes the interest and dividends they earn here. In acquiring the currency to invest here, they bid up the price of the U.S. dollar (in terms of other currencies). The more expensive dollar made imports cheaper in America, which contributed to lower prices overall.[2]

Long-Term & Short-Term Benefits

An economy with low tax rates tends to grow more rapidly than an economy with high tax rates. And the benefits of lower tax rates never end; they continue year after year, decade after decade.

On top of this, the economy receives a special tonic at the time the tax rates are reduced. The tonic comes from releasing all at

[2]The dollar finally peaked in 1985, after a 6-year rise. The peak arrived when American investments and products had become so expensive to foreigners that there no longer was an incentive for them to buy dollars.

once a backlog of business opportunities that had been shut out by high taxes. The lower rates make these projects feasible, and the large backlog of new enterprises can begin.

Business expansion plans are activated, new factories are built, and new products move from the drawing board to the market.

This extra tonic lasts only a few years, but it is powerful. In the early 1980s, it lessened the pain of getting off the inflation-recession seesaw. In the late 1980s, the second round of tax cuts kept prosperity alive despite the Federal Reserve's erratic monetary policies.

Protection Against Problems

The tax cuts also helped strengthen the economy against the problems that had accumulated in the 1960s and 1970s.

The new prosperity was good for banks. Many marginal banks were able to survive because the strong economy meant fewer bad loans, and because lower inflation rates led to lower interest rates.

The tax cuts kept the federal budget deficits from soaring into outer space. Because the economy grew so much, tax revenues rose an average of 7.3% per year from 1981 through 1988.[3]

Tax cuts may sound too good to be true, but there simply is no other factor that could have propelled the economy's strong recovery in the 1980s.

KEYNESIAN ECONOMICS?

It has been said that the tax cuts were Keynesian economics in disguise—that, by causing the federal deficits, the tax cuts simply created a quick fix for the economy that will have to be paid for later.

But there's a vast difference between Keynesian economics and cuts in tax rates.

[3]*Economic Indicators* (described on page 247), (May 1988), page 32.

The Keynesian approach was to stimulate the economy by getting more spendable income into the hands of individuals. How the money got there wasn't too important. You could use new government handouts not paid for by increased taxes. Or you could lower tax collections—even if tax *rates* remained unchanged—by increasing personal exemptions, or by granting tax credits or new (or accelerated) deductions.

But permanent cuts in tax *rates* are quite different. They might not even give people more money to spend right now. Instead, they operate by increasing the incentive to work and invest—which strengthens the economy permanently, rather than giving it a pep pill that will quickly wear off.

TAX INCREASE

Cuts in tax rates make the nation's *taxable income* larger—by increasing productivity and by reducing the value of tax avoidance. The government might collect as much or more revenue from the lower tax rates than it did when rates were higher.

There was hope in 1981 that the tax cuts would themselves eventually eliminate the federal deficits. If total government spending were held steady (which the election of President Reagan seemed to promise), rising federal revenues would catch up with spending, and the budget deficit would disappear.

As it turned out, revenues did rise dramatically—by 76% through 1988. But the politicians used the rising revenues as an opportunity to spend more, and the deficits grew.

Washington Wisdom

When the first tax cuts were proposed in 1981, government accountants were asked to estimate the effect of lower tax rates on government revenue. They made their estimate simply by applying the proposed new tax rates to the old levels of taxable income—without allowing for the increase in taxable income that the tax cuts were likely to produce.

The accountants saw lower revenues and larger deficits, and their estimates were widely publicized. Even though they have been proved wrong, their message has lingered; many people continue to believe a cut in tax rates means a cut in tax revenues, and hence larger deficits.

This misunderstanding is a boon for politicians who want the government to grow. It allows them to claim that only a tax increase can eliminate the budget deficit—even though the deficit would be wiped out just by returning in 1989 to the spending levels of 1986.

So long as the cause of the deficit remains obscure, the odds are heavy that a tax increase will be enacted in 1989 or 1990. If the increase is large enough, it almost certainly will detonate the economic time bomb.

Long-Term & Short-Term Harm

Every benefit that lower tax rates brought us in the 1980s would be swept away by a tax increase. Prosperity would be repealed.

Tax *cuts* permanently increase the incentive to invest and produce. And they provide an extra, brief tonic by giving the green light to opportunities that have been stalled by high tax rates.

Acting in reverse, a tax *increase* would place a permanent burden on the economy. And it would cause an immediate shock by slashing the after-tax profitability of many projects that otherwise would go forward.

A tax increase would worsen the recession that the Federal Reserve's tight-money policy of 1987 and 1988 is likely to trigger. And that would aggravate all three of the economy's major problems.

Banks would be hurt by a new wave of loan defaults, and by

the sharply higher interest rates that accompany the onset of a recession.

The Federal Reserve has already demonstrated that it would probably overreact to a recession—cranking up the money machine and flooding the country with new money.

And a tax increase probably wouldn't even end the federal deficits. If tax rates were raised by much, a damaged economy might yield less revenue for the government. If the tax increase were small enough, revenue might rise; but history suggests that this would merely invite the government to spend more—leaving the deficit unchanged or larger with a less productive economy.

And if the tax increase does trigger a recession, the government's automatic spending programs will escalate at the very time that revenues are falling. The deficits could easily balloon to $300 billion or $400 billion, and interest rates would go to the moon.

The economic time bomb would no longer be a metaphor. It would be a catastrophe.

7

The Stock Market Crash

As you know, the Dow Jones Industrial Average fell 508 points (22.6%) on October 19, 1987. After the flood of sell orders came a flood of predictions:

- A recession would begin by the spring of 1988, because the market crash made people feel less wealthy and they would curtail their spending.
- After a brief rally, the market would crash again early in 1988.
- The stock market would be extremely volatile for at least six months, because investors would be jumpy as a result of the crash.
- The Federal Reserve System would create new money at a furious pace in order to ward off a depression, so inflation couldn't be very far away.
- The president, Congress, and the public would finally wake up to the economy's terrible condition; we would all realize that something had to be done about the "twin deficits" (the federal budget deficit and the foreign trade deficit); and we'd all hang our heads and accept the "fiscal responsibility" of a tax increase.
- The lunacy on Wall Street finally would be ended by a prohibition of "program trading."

- The 5-year party of high living was over; now we would start paying the piper by accepting a lower standard of living.

A year after the crash, not one of these expectations had materialized.

Why not?

Because, despite what happened to individual investors, for the general economy the 1987 stock market crash was a non-event, a non-problem.

Many of the predictions of post-crash misery were just bad wishes—the hopes of frustrated partisans who for five years had been saying that Reaganomics would destroy the country. At last, a falling stock market gave them something to point to (even though they hadn't said earlier that a *rising* stock market was a sign of economic health).

In addition, the crash was frightening to many investors. They'd been told over and over that such a thing couldn't happen. When it *did* happen, people naturally worried over what might be coming next.

So forecasts of trouble to come found a receptive audience. Happily, none of the forecasts proved to be correct. No recession arrived in the spring of 1988, the crash didn't continue, and the stock market wasn't crippled by new regulations. In fact, except for investors who had bet too heavily on stocks, life went on as though there had never been a crash.

CAUSE OF THE CRASH

What caused the market to fall so far, so fast?

Most likely, the crash was caused by a combination of good times and erratic Federal Reserve monetary policy.

The same forces that revived the economy in the 1980s—lower tax rates, a steadier monetary policy in the early 1980s, and a more tolerant attitude toward the free market—caused the stock market to rise from 1982 through mid-1987.

As often happens in a bull market, stocks rose beyond a level justified solely by the immediate fundamentals (current book value, current earnings and dividends). The market was rising on expectations of *further* prosperity—on hope for the future. This made it vulnerable to any deterioration in confidence about the future, or anything that left investors with an immediate need for cash.

Meanwhile, the Federal Reserve in 1985 and 1986 was creating new money at a rapid rate. The money supply (M1 definition) rose 12% in 1985 and 17% in 1986—both considerably above the yearly average of 7% for the previous 10 years.

But at the beginning of 1987, the Fed suddenly slammed on the brakes. Throughout 1987, the money supply remained virtually flat. On October 19, 1987, the money supply was only 2% above where it had been on December 31, 1986.

Despite everything the Fed was supposed to have learned from the turbulent 1970s (covered in Chapter 2), it returned to its old stop-and-go monetary policy. For two years it drove 100 miles an hour; then, in January 1987, it stopped on a dime.

A good part of the new money the Fed creates finds its way into the stock market. This is because the Fed spends the money to buy bonds. Very often, the person or institution who sells bonds to the Fed will buy stocks with part of the money he receives. So the stock market can be especially sensitive to monetary growth.

With the Fed having made money very scarce in 1987, and with the possibility that stocks were overpriced, the stock market declined from August through October. For some reason, all the economic and psychological factors came together on October 19—and the market fell 508 points in one day.

What that reason was, I don't know. And I don't believe anyone really knows. Debates over the cause of the crash will continue for years, but will never be settled. Arguments continue today over the cause of the 1929 crash. ✳

SHortLy BeFoRe The crAsh FED CHAIRMAN GREENSPAN RAISED INTREST RATES. RIGHT AFTER The crAsh The Govt MADE FUNDS AVAIL To FINANCIAL ORGS FOR LIQUIDITY AND The INT.RATES LowEREd.

I don't really believe it's important to worry about what happened. It's far more productive to make sure you can't be hurt if something similar happens in the future. And then you can treat the next crash as a curiosity.[1]

DANGERS

The long-run danger of the crash lies in its power to inspire bogus reforms—proposals to fix a market that isn't broken.

The crash intensified calls to prohibit or limit insider trading, program trading, index futures, corporate takeovers, and more. Here we'll look at three examples of areas in which the reformers hope to improve upon the free market.

The zeal for reform may lead to new laws or regulations that are bad for the investment markets and bad for the economy.

INSIDER TRADING

Individuals trading with "inside" information have been accused of cheating honest investors during the bull market.

The complaint is sometimes presented as a plea for a "level playing field"—whereon all investors have the same opportunities. Using information that others lack is considered somehow to be unfair.

But the concept of a "level playing field" makes little sense when applied to the investment markets, and in fact the idea reveals a lack of understanding of how markets work.

Investors aren't necessarily competing against one another.

[1]In Part II, I'll discuss ways to insulate yourself from a crash while remaining in a position to profit from a bull market.

And investment markets aren't "zero sum games" in which one player can win only at another player's expense. If they were, they would have faded away years ago—soon after the opening of casinos that provide free drinks while you gamble.

Two people exchanging money and stock are no different from two people exchanging money and doughnuts. Each transaction is arranged because it pleases both parties. We would never think of calling the buyer and seller of doughnuts "competitors"—nor would we attempt to decide which one was the "winner" and which one the "loser."

If someone buys a stock at $30 and sells it at $42 to someone who later sells it at $51, who is the winner and who is the loser?

The answer is self-evident. Each is a winner, and each benefits the other—just as though they were dealing in doughnuts.

Outsider Trading

But what if one of them had "inside" information? By tilting the playing field in his own favor, did he hurt the other investor?

Let's suppose Mr. Outsider bought his stock in April at $30 and then decided to sell on June 5. Mr. Insider, who knew that something important was going to happen on June 12, bought the stock at $42 from Mr. Outsider. On June 12, the expected event occurred, the price jumped to $51, and Mr. Insider sold for a quick profit.

The fairness buff believes that Mr. Insider made his profit at the expense of Mr. Outsider. But he assumes that Mr. Outsider sold only because Mr. Insider wanted to buy.

In fact, Mr. Outsider sold for his own reasons. If he hadn't sold to Mr. Insider, he would have sold to someone else. Mr. Insider's presence simply added one additional buyer bidding for Mr. Outsider's stock—which may have given Mr. Outsider a slightly better price at which to sell.

The fairness buff believes that, to behave fairly, Mr. Insider should have made his inside information public before he bought the stock.

But if Mr. Insider had been required to tell what he knew before buying, he wouldn't have bought at all—since his revelation would have driven the price of the stock up before he could buy. So Mr. Insider still would have kept quiet, and Mr. Outsider still would have sold his stock at $42.

Mr. Insider didn't cost Mr. Outsider anything. So how would a level playing field make Mr. Outsider any better off?[2]

But perhaps we're forgetting someone. We've overlooked Mr. Latecomer—the poor guy who bought Mr. Insider's stock at $51, possibly at its peak price.

Mr. Insider didn't create the event that caused the stock to rise to $51; he only profited from it. The stock would have gone up with or without Mr. Insider—and Mr. Latecomer's transaction would have been no more profitable without Mr. Insider in the picture.

Fair Trade

The essence of the anti-insider-trading argument is that no one should have help that you and I don't have. But why not? Everyone's situation is different, and it will always be so.

Some people have better computers, subscribe to more newsletters, get phone calls in the middle of the night warning them of market crashes, have a better feel for the market, get better executions from their brokers, receive free advice from their brothers-in-law, and in many other ways enjoy competitive advantages. Should we subject everyone to brain surgery in order to equalize opportunity?

To the best of my knowledge, no one has advanced an argument

[2]Even if Mr. Outsider sells at a loss, the principle is the same. Without Mr. Insider to sell to, his loss would be the same or greater.

to show how you and I would be better off with insider trading prohibited. The desire to ban insider trading seems to be motivated more by envy than by a passion for justice.

Heard in the Alley

The case of Foster Winans enables us to see who may be harmed in an insider-trading situation.

Mr. Winans wrote the "Heard on the Street" column for *The Wall Street Journal.* The column reported opinions, favorable and unfavorable, held by Wall Street traders about individual stocks.

He apparently became involved in a scheme whereby stocks were bought or sold in advance of their being mentioned favorably or unfavorably in Mr. Winans's column. He and his coconspirators supposedly profited from inside information.

If their profits came at any investors' expense, it must be those who bought a stock after it was mentioned in an article—because the conspirators' advance purchase would have made the stock slightly more expensive than it would have been otherwise.

But those investors would have bigger problems than that.

A basic investment rule is: Don't buy an investment at the time good news is published about it. Its price probably reflects the good news already, and if the future doesn't live up to today's expectations, the price could drop.

Investors who expect to get rich buying stocks singled out in a newspaper read by 2 million people need to be protected from much more than insider trading.

Employers & Employees

Since *The Wall Street Journal* is a serious newspaper, its management was quite upset when it discovered what was happening. Obviously, Mr. Winans was subverting the value of the column to readers. And the problem could get much worse. For example, he might seek out stocks that are thinly traded and thus are more readily influenced by a newspaper plug.

And so one would expect the *Journal* to have rules about stock trading by employees and leaking of information—as in fact it does. If it didn't, it would lose the confidence of its readers—and then lose the readers themselves.

The situation is similar for law firms, accounting firms, investment banks, and other companies whose employees might be aware of sensitive information about impending mergers, takeovers, and other corporate secrets. It's bad for business to become known as a company that can't keep a secret. Look at the CIA.

So most such companies require employees to sign secrecy agreements. And there we find the only insider-trading "scandal" that truly is scandalous.

The injured party isn't an investor who rolls down a tilted playing field. The victim is the company whose employee has violated his contract—whether the employee is a lawyer, a broker, or just someone who overheard a conversation.

In every case, the culprit was the individual who divulged information that he had promised not to reveal. And the victim is the company he worked for.

The crime is one of theft by an employee, and it's properly a matter between an employer and his employee—not a crime committed against investors, who were affected only incidentally by the act.

Since laws already exist to deal with employees who steal money, merchandise, and information, why do we need federal storm troopers to regulate what insiders do?

Victims?

Crusaders are always on the lookout for a new class of victims—whose protection demands new legislation.

The latest victim they aim to protect is the investor who must compete with investors who are better prepared or equipped. After all, a lone investor is helpless. How can he hope to compete with the rich insiders of this world? We must have agencies to protect the "little guy."

But we already have agencies that protect the "little guy." They're called "mutual funds." And there also are pension funds, limited partnerships, money managers, investment periodicals, and (dare I say it?) books about investing. All these things offer professional help to solitary investors.

If someone loses money consistently in the investment markets, it isn't because he keeps getting taken by insiders, arbitragers, market-making specialists, floor traders, scalpers, raiders, or dark-eyed gypsies. It's because he's careless or lazy or wishful or reckless or completely unknowledgeable about investments.

No matter what laws are passed, he'll continue to lose money until he learns at least a little about managing risk.

Pandora's Box

The grandstanders on Capitol Hill hoped to capitalize on the insider-trading excitement. It wasn't Watergate, but they did their best with what they had. Attempts were made to stir up support for legislation to put everyone on an equal footing—as determined by the same 535 people who exempt themselves from the laws they pass to restrain the rest of us. (No penalties were proposed for exploiting inside political information.)

If they succeed someday, the result will be less efficient markets, higher costs for trading and investing, wider spreads between buying and selling prices, more legal fees, and the suppression of information that otherwise would be available.

But none of these costs will come with a label saying, "Caused by the prosecution of inside traders."

PRICE LIMITS

The most straightforward proposal for avoiding market crashes was to make them illegal.

Specifically, the proposal called for a system of daily price limits. A stock's price would be allowed to move only so far each day from the previous day's close. For example, if the limit were 20%, a stock that closed yesterday at a price of 50 could not rise today above 60 or fall below 40.

If a stock has a bad day, and no one is willing to buy at 40 or higher, trading will come to a halt. Many people might be happy to sell at the legal minimum of 40, but no one will want to buy at that price—and no one will be allowed to buy or sell at any price below 40.

The next day, the 20% limit will cause the minimum and maximum to be 32 and 48 (20% below and above 40). There might be no trading for days, while investors wait for the price limits to catch up to the reality of market conditions.

Daily limits already apply on most U.S. futures exchanges—for commodity, currency, and financial futures contracts, but not for stock index futures.

Cooling Off

The principal argument for price limits is that they provide a cooling-off period. The price can drop or rise only so far—and then trading halts. After a day or so, the general fear or enthusiasm may have waned, and trading can resume—without the price having reached an extreme.

Trading limits might accomplish that, but what would be the benefit? Where is the virtue in making a given stock (or the market as a whole) hide in the closet when we don't like the way it's behaving? Falling stock prices may not be welcome, but are they lewd or obscene? Should "Wall $treet Week" be kept off the air until the children are in bed?

Since no one is ever *forced* to buy or sell, anyone can declare his own trading halt simply by taking a vacation. If he prefers, he can wait forever for the price of his stock to rebound. He doesn't need a law or an exchange rule for that.

But if he does want to sell, perhaps because he needs the money badly, he's out of luck when trading is halted. Trading limits merely prevent investors from doing what they want to do—and, as such, are more likely to drive investors away from the market than lure them in.

In March 1980, shortly after the price of silver had peaked at $50, price limits prevented trading in New York silver futures contracts for 20 market days. The unregulated cash price (the true market price) was below the exchange's limits every day. The minimum price limit was lower day after day, but the market price remained out of reach.

If you owned a silver investment outside the futures market, free from the daily price limits, you were able to sell early during the drop—at around $30. But if price limits kept you locked into a futures contract, your first chance to sell came at around $13. And, to this day, the market hasn't seen $30 again.

Increased Volatility

Ironically, price limits wouldn't make the market less volatile. The fear of being trapped in a sinking ship would make prices *more* volatile.

If you're nervous about a stock you own, and you see the price falling toward the daily limit, you may decide to sell in a hurry—in order to get out before trading is halted by law. As you and others try to sell before the limit is reached, the price will drop more rapidly. Nothing creates a panic more surely than a locked exit.

Without a price limit, you might have been willing to wait and see—knowing you were free to sell whenever your patience and tenacity were exhausted. But with daily limits, you're pressured to sell before the law makes your stock unsalable—knowing that once the price limit is reached, your holdings might be frozen for days.

The mere presence of daily limits will amplify price declines.

PROGRAM TRADING

When the stock market crashed, the favorite whipping boys were program traders—investors who use computer programs to tell them when to buy and sell.

Some large investors (such as mutual funds) use these programs to determine when to implement portfolio insurance (buying put options or selling short an index futures contract) when a market decline causes the value of their stocks to fall below some predetermined point.[3]

Program trading also is used by arbitragers, who seek to profit when the value of an index futures contract differs from the value of the stocks that make up the index. The arbitragers perform a service to other investors in the market—even though, as with all investors, they are motivated by profit alone.

Without arbitrage, people who buy stock index futures couldn't be assured that the price of the futures contract would always reflect the state of the underlying stock index. Without that assurance, there's no point in trading the futures contract—since it would have no tie to the real world. The futures contract would

---

[3] A *put option* is a contract that allows you to sell a stock at a guaranteed price, if you choose to do so, anytime until an expiration date. Owning one allows you to hold on to a stock without worrying so much about its price dropping. An *index futures contract* is an investment instrument whose value depends on the movement in a stock index (such as the Standard & Poor's 500 index); it must be sold and settled by an expiration date. *Selling short* is a bet that the index will go down; if the market does drop, the gain from selling short will offset losses incurred in stocks you own.

be an absurdity—like a market for buying and selling half-acre lots on Mars.

Benefits of Index Futures

It is said often that stock index futures themselves serve no more economic purpose than a blackjack table in a casino. But in fact they offer many services to investors.

An investor fearing a temporary price decline might use index futures as an easy and inexpensive way of neutralizing his position in stocks without having to sell the stocks themselves.

Another investor might use an index contract to acquire a diversified position in far more stocks than his stock budget could purchase directly. Or he might use it as a simple way of selling the overall market short.

Some investors use futures contracts purely as a speculation. The presence of speculators makes the market much larger than one containing only long-term investors. The result is greater liquidity and stability—making it easier for all investors to buy and sell when they want to.

Benefits of Speculative Instruments

Critics sometimes sneer at stock index futures contracts, index options, and the like as mere gambling instruments—because such contracts are settled entirely in cash, with no stock ever changing hands.

This is a very shortsighted view. All investment instruments perform a service to the economy, but sometimes you have to look for the connection.

For example, put options on stock indices allow you to hedge the stocks you own against a potential decline. The ability to do this makes it less risky to buy stocks in the first place. And the more that people invest in stocks, the more capital can be raised for new business ventures—because potential investors know there's a liquid market available whenever they decide to sell.

When you want to buy a put option, there might not be another investor who—at precisely the same moment—wants to *sell* that option. Fortunately, there are speculators—gamblers—in the market who, for a price, will gladly take the other side of the transaction you want. Without them, prices would be much more volatile and the investment markets much less efficient.

People who gamble in options or futures contracts may care little for the welfare of the country—or even for *your* welfare. But, whatever their motives, they provide a useful service to you, the investment markets, and the nation.

THE MORE THINGS CHANGE . . .

After every crash, new laws and rules are created to prevent a repetition. But, somehow, another crash occurs sooner or later—leading to the imposition of more laws and rules—which somehow don't prevent yet another crash from coming along eventually.

It is the same in the investment markets as elsewhere in society. The battle against "sin" is never-ending. Every new law is promoted as essential and decisive, but somehow it fails to win the battle—and new laws are heaped on top of the old ones, which are never repealed. And so the pile grows bigger and bigger.

Whenever there's a crisis, everything is investigated except the question of whether the crisis was caused by too many laws.

The enemies of society aren't the program traders, the inside traders, the arbitragers, the big brokers, the institutions, the speculators, the exchanges, or the corporate raiders.

The enemies are the people who can't leave well enough alone—who can't let other people run their own lives—who can't stop meddling in things that have nothing to do with them.

Today the financial system is too weak to tolerate too much

meddling. Impositions on the stock market are impositions on the ability to raise capital, to start new ventures, and to create new jobs. Regulating the stock market is as dangerous as regulating the economy itself.

Second Chance

When the excitement died down after the 1987 crash, and people could see that none of the dire predictions had come to pass, the interest in new laws and regulations died out.

I doubt that this would happen if there were a second crash, however. There would be weeping and wailing that we had been given one chance to "clean up our act" and we'd flunked it. The cry would be that nothing less than a thorough housecleaning at the stock exchange would save us. But the housecleaning would bring on an economic crisis much faster than would the crash itself.

For example, price limits that cause trading to halt might be imposed—causing investors to panic as the limits are approached. The trading halt also might be frightening to people *outside* the investment markets—more frightening than a large price drop would be.

Suppose that bad news about a big bank caused the Dow Jones to drop 150 points one morning. If there were a 200-point daily trading limit, the fear of reaching that limit might cause investors to sell in a hurry. The 200-point limit might be reached by late morning—causing the stock market to be closed for the rest of the day.

How will the event be reported? Do you think that all news reports will be calm, accurate, and reasonable? And how will people in general—many of whom see the stock market as a place of dangerous mystery—react?

When non-investors hear that the stock market is closed because of problems at a major bank, they might decide to play it safe and get their money out of their own banks. The government-imposed trading limit—the cooling-off period, the chance to calm the markets—might itself cause a general run on the nation's banks.

Because the market crash of October 1987 *didn't* cause panic or problems in the economy, you would think it might be better just to leave things alone.

8

The Trade Deficit

The trade deficit may be the most seductive non-problem we're being urged to solve.

The issue is too tempting for the politicians to resist. Keeping imports out of the U.S. doesn't seem to hurt anyone but a few nonvoting foreigners, while it visibly saves the jobs of thousands of grateful, voting Americans.

The damage done by trade barriers may be invisible to the politicians, but it is real nonetheless. Interference with foreign trade disrupts our own economy as much as, or more than, it hurts foreigners. Our economy *is* trade. Anything that gets in the way of buying and selling gets in the way of prosperity, and makes it harder for the economy to overcome its real problems.

Imposing restrictions to fix the trade deficit is like pounding on the economic time bomb with a hammer.

WHAT IS THE TRADE DEFICIT?

The U.S. foreign trade balance is calculated by adding up the value of all products sold by Americans to foreign customers, and subtracting the total value of all products purchased by Americans from foreign suppliers.

If the result is a positive number, we have a trade surplus. A negative number means a trade deficit.[1]

A trade deficit means that we collectively are buying more products from foreigners than they are buying from us. A trade *surplus* would mean that we were selling more products to foreigners than they were selling to us.

The graph on page 101 shows the yearly trade balance from 1790 through 1988. To keep the amounts in perspective, each year's balance is shown as a percentage of that year's Gross National Product (an estimate of America's production of goods and services).

As you can see, America had trade deficits in most of the years of the 19th century—the years in which the U.S. economy was growing very rapidly. Late in the century, the trade account shifted to a surplus—and remained that way for almost every year until the 1970s.

In 1971 the U.S. had a trade deficit for the first time since 1893, but it was only $2 billion. Small deficits continued through 1976.

From 1977 through 1982, the deficits were more significant—about $30 billion per year. In 1983 the deficit moved upward again—to $67 billion—and then continued upward year by year to $113 billion, $122 billion, and $145 billion. In 1987 it reached $160 billion.[2]

Politicians enjoy talking about the trade deficit. It gives them a chance to appear knowledgeable about a grave and complex matter—one that also can be couched in patriotic terms. They argue that the United States has lost its competitiveness; that

[1]Payments such as interest, dividends, fees for services, insurance premiums, and royalties aren't considered in the trade balance. Along with the trade balance, they go into the *current account balance.* And investments—stocks, bonds, bank deposits, and the like—that cross national boundaries are counted in the *capital account balance.* Our concern here is only with the trade balance—which is the issue that has been receiving public attention the past few years.

[2]All trade figures are estimates by the U.S. government, and the margin of error is so large that any small deficit may actually have been a surplus, and vice versa. Sources of the data are given on page 292.

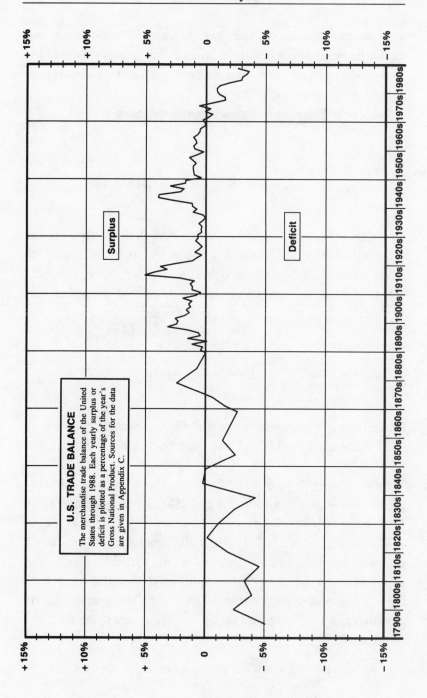

U.S. TRADE BALANCE

The merchandise trade balance of the United States through 1988. Each yearly surplus or deficit is plotted as a percentage of the year's Gross National Product. Sources for the data are given in Appendix C.

Surplus

Deficit

we're becoming a second-class nation, trailing behind Japan and the European countries; that the trade deficit proves we are living on debt, consuming more than we produce; and that imports are putting Americans out of work.

But, in fact, the trade deficit is a non-problem.

WHY THERE IS A TRADE DEFICIT

The trade deficits of the 1970s may have resulted mostly from the rising value of imported oil. But the larger trade deficits of the 1980s most likely were caused by the prosperity we've experienced, and by the reductions in tax rates that propelled that prosperity.

Greater Prosperity

Rising prosperity tends to feed a trade deficit, because people have more income with which to purchase everything, including imports.

From late 1982 through early 1988, the American economy grew at the unusually strong rate of 4.2% per year, after averaging 2.2% per year over the previous 10 years.[3]

Meanwhile, most other industrial countries were barely growing at all. European countries in particular were still mired in the kind of economic quicksand that had held back the United States during the 1970s. Here are average yearly growth rates for the other major industrial countries for 1982 through 1987:

[3] *Economic Indicators* (described on page 247), June 1988 and January 1984, page 2.

Average Yearly Change in Gross National Product, 1982–87

Canada	+ 4.6%
France	+ 1.7%
Germany	+ 2.3%
Great Britain	+ 3.2%
Italy	+ 2.4%
Japan	+ 4.0%
Sweden	+ 2.5%
Switzerland	+ 2.3%[4]

European governments didn't—and still don't—encourage the kind of economic growth we have become used to in America. Not only are European tax rates much higher, but economic regulation of private companies is far more extensive.

Because the European economies were growing slowly, their demand for American products also grew slowly. But America was prosperous enough to buy products from all over the world.

Investment Opportunities in the U.S.

From 1981 onward, lower U.S. tax rates made the United States a more attractive place in which to invest.

And foreign investors were reassured by the rapid fall in inflation. They could purchase dollar-denominated bonds of U.S. companies with less risk that future inflation would drive interest rates upward and push the dollar downward.

To invest in the U.S., foreigners first had to exchange their own currencies for U.S. dollars. This foreign demand for dollars pushed up the price of the U.S. dollar in the foreign currency markets.

In Germany, for example, between 1980 and 1985 the price of

[4]*International Financial Statistics* (described on page 247), June 1988, lines 99b.*p* and 99a.*r*.

a U.S. dollar more than doubled—from 1.68 German marks to 3.45 marks. When the prices of American products were translated from dollars into marks, they had become much more expensive. The same was true in every other major country. American products became costly all over the world, and foreigners reacted to higher prices by buying fewer American goods.

A more expensive U.S. dollar meant that foreign currencies were cheaper for Americans to acquire. The price of a German mark fell from $.60 down to $.29—making German products much cheaper for Americans to buy. The strong dollar allowed Americans to enjoy international bargains—and so, naturally, they bought much more from foreigners.

Curing the Trade Deficit

Of course, it would be easy enough to cure the trade deficit. All the U.S. government has to do is outlaw imports. Or it could increase its subsidies to exporters.

The result would be fewer choices for the American consumer, higher prices for everyone, a bigger federal deficit, and perhaps a second Great Depression to boot.

But at least we would have done something about the trade deficit.

TWO-WAY TRADE

When foreigners earn dollars by selling their products in the U.S., they either spend the dollars in the U.S. or trade them to other foreigners who want to spend them here. Were it not for the Americans who buy imports, no foreigners would have dollars with which to buy American products.

Thus, when imports increase, so does the amount of money available to foreigners to purchase U.S. products. The Americans who purchase cars from Japan and shoes from Italy and shirts from Hong Kong and wine from France are making possible sales *to* foreigners of American wheat, American airplanes, American computers, American medical instruments, and American movies.

Of course, the total of imports doesn't equal the total of exports every day, or even every year—which is why there can be a trade deficit (or surplus) to talk about.

But the dollars that don't come back to buy American products will come back to purchase U.S. stocks, U.S. bonds, U.S. real estate, U.S. businesses, and U.S. factories. The dollars *have* to come back here; there's nothing else a foreign seller can do with them. He can't spend them in Tokyo, Seoul, or Frankfurt; so he has to trade them to someone who will use them in the United States.

LOST JOBS

It's true that foreign competition causes some American businesses to lose sales they otherwise would make. And when competition increases in a particular industry, some employees in that industry lose their jobs.

It is sad to see any business go bankrupt or any worker lose his job. And when foreign competition seems to be the cause, it's easy to think we'd all be better off by shutting out imports.

But competition of *any* kind can lead to change. An American company *without* foreign competition can go out of business— leaving workers unemployed—because it isn't offering customers what they need or want most.

Often a company goes out of business because someone has found a way to produce a better product, or produce the same product at a lower price. That "someone" might be a foreign company or another American company. Outlawing foreign competition won't protect us from the facts of life.

How Many Jobs Have Been Lost?

Imports eliminate jobs in industries in which foreign companies are especially efficient. But they don't reduce the overall number of jobs in the United States. Instead, imports cause U.S. workers to move from one industry to another.

The industries that benefit from imports are the industries where foreigners spend the dollars they earned selling products to us. Farm employment, for example, is greater than it would be without imports—since American farmers are large-scale exporters. And employment in the aircraft industry is encouraged by imports because the aircraft industry sells large chunks of its output to foreigners who have earned dollars.

And industries throughout the economy benefit from capital invested by foreigners—invested in amounts that match the trade deficit.

Hindering foreign imports would save some U.S. jobs but eliminate others—probably more jobs than would be saved. Free trade across international borders doesn't reduce the total number of jobs; it eliminates some jobs in some industries and creates jobs in other industries—usually resulting in a net increase in jobs overall.

Free trade expands everyone's market—creating more opportunities to sell and giving more choices and better prices to buyers—so that every country that welcomes imports is more prosperous.

How many Americans have the Japanese and Germans put out of work? From 1982 through early 1988—the years of the largest trade deficits—U.S. employment grew rapidly, while employment in most other countries was stable or shrinking:

Change in Employment, 1982–88

Canada	+10.5%
France	− 4.1%
Germany	− 3.0%
Great Britain	+ 2.9%
Italy	−12.8%
Japan	+ 1.7%
Sweden	+ 1.8%
Switzerland	+ 7.6%
United States	+15.6%[5]

A great many of the new American jobs are with companies financed by foreign investors—using dollars they earned selling to customers in the United States.

Seen & Unseen

There's a big political difference between the jobs lost to foreign competition and the jobs and other benefits gained through foreign trade.

The lost jobs are often concentrated in highly visible industries—such as steel, automobiles, or consumer electronics. But the benefits are dispersed throughout the American economy. The pain is obvious, but the gains are almost invisible.

Where the benefits are concentrated in major industries, such as aircraft or computers, the skill of the management or the diligence of the workers will get the credit—while the losses in industries hit by foreign competition are blamed solely on the foreigners.

You will hear again and again how automakers, steelworkers, and textile workers have been hurt by imports. But how often have you heard Boeing or IBM attribute its export profits to the imports

[5]*International Financial Statistics* (described on page 247), June 1988, various country pages, line 67.

of cars or steel or shirts? But it is those imports that provide foreigners with the dollars to pay for jumbo jets and computers.

And while we've often seen unemployed steelworkers on the evening news, we seldom see consumers rejoicing over the lower prices that come with free trade.

We hear about the pain but not the benefits of foreign trade, and so the trade deficit is an attractive political issue. A politician is "compassionate" if he vows to stop the "exporting of jobs"—even though his compassion will hurt more Americans than it helps.

DUMPING

The politician sometimes justifies tariffs and quotas by accusing foreigners of cutthroat competition—selling products in the U.S. at prices "below cost."

But, of course, most U.S. companies sell at prices below their costs at one time or another. They may do so to introduce a new product, or to gain a customer's attention with one product in order to sell him other products at a profit. American companies also may sell a product at less than cost when they discover they have too much of it, and can get rid of the excess only by selling at a loss, or when they are pinched for cash.

It's easy to understand why U.S. companies sometimes sell at prices below their costs. But below-cost sales by foreign companies are thought to be predatory—perhaps because the seller is so foreign.

Foreigners have also been accused of dumping products at prices below cost in order to destroy their American competitors and make us dependent on foreign sources.

But we've long been dependent on foreign sources for many things—even essential materials such as platinum, tin, and nickel. No nation is self-sufficient, and you wouldn't like living in the countries that have come the closest—countries such as Romania, Uganda, Bulgaria, and Cambodia.

RETALIATION

The opponents of foreign trade say "we must have trade that is fair as well as free."

They point out that the Japanese government makes it difficult for Americans to sell in Japan. And they cite the high tariffs (taxes) that many nations impose on products coming from America. So, we are told, we should keep other nations' products out of the U.S. until they open their borders to ours.

Why? If the Japanese government (or any other) makes it difficult for its citizens to buy American products, why should we "get even" by refusing to buy Japanese products? What does one have to do with the other?

We buy Japanese products because they enhance our standard of living. If we outlaw Japanese products, we hurt ourselves as much as we hurt the Japanese. So what would we gain?

I buy a Japanese car if it represents the best value for me—not because Goro Yamamoto agrees to buy my book.

The Forgotten Consumer

By granting our own government the right to determine which foreign products have been priced "fairly" or which countries treat American exporters "justly," we give up our freedom to make our own buying decisions.

"Free but fair trade" sounds so reasonable and evenhanded. But in practice it means that consumers must forgo what they want and buy substitutes at higher prices.

When foreign trade becomes a political issue, it is decided in favor of those who can best influence politicians. It's profitable for a shoe producer to spend a million dollars lobbying to get foreign shoes priced out of the U.S. market—so that he can sell an additional million pairs at higher prices. But a consumer has no incentive to go to Washington to try to save $10 on a single pair of shoes.

Because the producer has a much larger and more concentrated stake, the consumer's interest is invariably sacrificed—even as politicians and reformers claim to speak on the consumer's behalf.[6]

A CASE OF SELF-DESTRUCTION

A recent problem in the computer industry illustrates the mess that government can make of foreign trade.

The United States is the world's leading exporter of computers. An essential component in any computer is its "memory"—which is composed, in large part, of electronic chips. A few American companies make these chips, but most of the memory chips used by independent American computer makers come from Japan.

In the mid-1980s, Japanese manufacturers found that they were producing more memory chips than they could sell. So in 1986 they slashed their prices drastically in order to reduce their inventories. Prodded by U.S. chip makers, the U.S. government ruled that the Japanese were "dumping" their chips in the U.S.—selling them at prices below their own costs.

Apparently the Reagan administration wanted somehow to intervene and still be able to stand up for free trade. So, instead of putting high tariffs or low quotas on the foreign chips, it worked out a "voluntary" agreement with the Japanese government. The Japanese would restrict exports of chips to the U.S.—and the Japanese government would take over the marketing of the chips, so that no Japanese company could sell more than its quota.

As a result, the volume of Japanese memory chips coming into America dropped sharply.

---

[6]Those who call themselves *consumer advocates* "help" the consumer by trying to outlaw products that consumers want, and by pressuring government to force changes in products that make them less attractive to consumers.

Unintended Consequences

The U.S. chip manufacturers were pleased by the arrangement, which allowed them to raise their prices. But they couldn't produce enough chips to offset the shortage.

And so American computer makers were left without chips. Computer production fell, computer prices rose, and introductions of new, larger-memory computers were postponed or canceled altogether.

The agreement imposed upon Japan for the benefit of America turned out to be good for Japan and bad for America. While American computer production suffered, the agreement turned the Japanese chip manufacturers into a government-sponsored cartel. The government-enforced production limits allowed Japanese manufacturers to increase their prices and profits, without fear that any competitor would undersell them.

The outcome was similar to what happened when the Japanese government agreed to "voluntary" quotas on the exporting of Japanese cars to the United States. American consumers wound up paying substantially higher prices for Japanese *and* American cars—while Japanese carmakers divided up a smaller market with much higher profits.

In each case—memory chips and automobiles—the agreement was initiated by the American government, supposedly to benefit Americans.[7]

HOW WE CAN BE HURT

The chip and car fiascos illustrate the dangers inherent in "doing something" about the trade deficit. Computers and cars became more expensive, and the growth of the American computer indus-

[7]Cartels in which producers agree to raise prices and restrict output seldom succeed for very long. The members cheat (to take advantage of the higher prices), and the high prices invite competition from nonmembers of the cartel and from the makers of products that can be substituted. Cartels are successful only when governments enforce restrictive production quotas and keep outsiders from competing.

try was severely hindered when an essential source of supply was cut off.

But much worse will happen if the government restricts imports in general.

With foreigners selling less to us, they'll have fewer dollars to invest in the U.S. The stream of investments from abroad that has kept interest rates low and created so many new American jobs will slow to a trickle.

The shutting off of essential foreign supplies will weaken many American manufacturers.

And trade restrictions will worsen each of the three danger areas of the economy—potential inflation, the budget deficit, and a sick banking industry.

Inflation would be encouraged by trade restrictions. Consumers no longer could buy the lowest-priced products. And American producers of similar products, freed from foreign competition, would lose an incentive to hold their costs and prices in check.

Trade barriers would worsen the federal budget deficit. The reductions in foreign products, foreign investment, and supplies for American manufacturers would lead to lower corporate profits and lower personal incomes—and hence to lower tax revenues.

And the trade restrictions would aggravate the problems of the banking industry. The entire world economy would slow down, depriving third-world countries of the export earnings needed to pay their debts to U.S. banks. It would be hard to think of a more violent shock to the banks than the refusal of third-world governments to pay anything further on their loans.

And that wouldn't be the end of the story. The trade issue won't be decided by American politicians alone. If the U.S. puts up high tariff walls, other governments will undoubtedly "get even" by restricting imports from the United States. With American exports shrinking as rapidly as imports, the trade deficit would still be with us—as big as life.

But we wouldn't be nearly as well off as we are now. The reduction of both exports and imports would constrict the American economy, reduce our choices as consumers, and lower our standard of living. Consumer and industrial prices would be higher, the federal deficit would be worse, and the banks would be in even deeper trouble.

1988 Bill

In 1988, Congress passed a protectionist trade bill and the president signed it. Fortunately, the bill's final version had only a few punitive provisions, and there were even a few sections that enhanced free trade. Apparently the purpose of the bill was to allow politicians to say that they had done something concrete about the trade deficit.

However, the protectionists didn't get what they wanted, and so they'll probably be back again in 1989—looking for more. And if the trade deficit doesn't shrink, it will serve as justification for a harsher bill.

THE TIME BOMB

The American economy is a time bomb—ticking away toward an explosion.

One shock that could trigger the bomb would be an attempt to "fix" the trade deficit by restricting imports. Remember the damage done to the computer industry, and try to imagine it repeated in dozens of industries across the American economy.

Economists disagree about many things. But there are two questions upon which there is almost unanimous agreement among economists of all political persuasions—left, right, and center. One of those principles is that free, unhampered trade among nations is good for everyone. (The other is that minimum-wage laws cause unemployment—the higher the minimum, the greater the unemployment.)

The trade deficit is a non-problem. Left alone, it will disappear on its own someday—probably because it has already made the U.S. dollar cheap enough for foreigners to buy more American products.

But the disappearance of the trade deficit won't make us any better off. The trade balance is merely a statistical curiosity.

To an individual who loses his job to foreign competition, the pain is real. We can't expect him to listen to a dissertation on free trade. Even if he agrees with the concept in principle, he probably can think of a reason for considering himself an exception.

But the people in public life—the politicians and journalists—who exploit the trade deficit as a problem to be fixed should know better. They're showing their ignorance of the most elementary economic principles. Or else they're showing their *disregard* for those principles—because they would rather use the trade deficit for professional or political ends.

In either case, the situation is dangerous. The politicians and journalists should be trying to defuse the time bomb. Instead, they're playing with it.

9

Confessions of a Debtor Nation

If you don't read *Time, Newsweek, Business Week, Forbes, Barron's, The Wall Street Journal, The New York Times,* or any other daily newspaper, or watch television, or listen to the radio, you might not have heard that the United States has become a "debtor nation." For the first time since the 19th century, it seems that Americans collectively owe more money to foreigners than foreigners owe to Americans.

This terrible stigma has been cited by anyone wishing to prove that "we're living beyond our means"—piling up debts and bills that our children and grandchildren will have to pay off by toiling in workhouses.

But the "debtor nation" label is a non-problem. It's a misnomer, it isn't accurate, and it wouldn't matter if it were.

What the Figures Mean

The claim is that the U.S. has become a "debtor nation"—that the debts owed to foreigners by U.S. individuals, corporations, and governments collectively amount to more than what foreigners owe to Americans.

So you might imagine that the figures quoted are figures concerning debt. But they aren't.

The official figures sweep together international investments of all kinds—stocks, bonds, real estate, businesses, almost everything. So part of our "debts" to foreigners are the American stocks, bonds, real estate, and businesses owned by foreigners—even though foreigners have no way of presenting these "debts" for payment.

Where Have All the Boosters Gone?

What the figures mean, if they're accurate, is that foreigners have invested more in the United States than Americans have invested abroad.

Is that so bad? What town in the U.S. doesn't have a chamber of commerce that tries to attract outside investors to its fair city? Should the town fathers be sorry when they succeed?

If money from elsewhere will build factories and provide new employment, should we worry ourselves to death that the money comes from people who don't watch "Monday Night Football"?

Cooking the Books

Don't bother answering those rhetorical questions, because the "debt" figures aren't accurate anyway—or even close to being so.

Foreigners have indeed been investing heavily in the U.S. in the 1980s, just as Americans invested so much overseas in the 1950s, 1960s, and 1970s. But the passage of time makes the bookkeeper's "debt balance" meaningless—because, even 30 or 40 years after the fact, every investment is still being counted at its original cost.

This means that the older, American investments abroad are counted at fractions of current market values—while the newer, foreign investments here are being counted at values closer to actual worth. If all the investments were counted at current market values, we probably would find that Americans own a good deal more overseas than foreigners own here.

In fact, in 1987 Americans received $100 billion in investment income from abroad, while foreigners received only $85 billion in investment income from the U.S. It's hard to imagine that Americans owe more than they are owed, yet receive more in interest and dividends than they pay.

When fees and royalties from direct investments are added in, the disparity is $11 billion greater—meaning that Americans receive $26 billion more than they pay to foreigners.[1]

The Selling of America

You and I might be satisfied with this explanation, but the handwringers are not.

Even if America isn't a net debtor *yet,* they say, it has been moving in that direction in recent years. We are allowing foreigners to own too much of America—a dangerous situation.

But why is it dangerous? For decades, Americans have owned large chunks of foreign companies, billions in foreign bonds, and kilometers of foreign real estate. In fact, it used to be a big issue in Europe that Americans were buying up the continent.

Now the pendulum has swung the other way, because America in the 1980s became a much more attractive place to invest. As a result, Americans see less reason to invest overseas, and foreigners are more eager to invest here.

This is simply a replay of what happened in the 19th century, when a healthy, free, rapidly growing U.S. economy attracted capital and immigrants from all over the world.

But the alarmists worry that foreigners will take control of major American corporations away from us. But whom do they

[1]*Economic Indicators* (described on page 247), May 1988, page 36. Be aware that all these statistics are only crude estimates made by the government.

mean by "us"? Do you control IBM and General Motors now? Will you have less clout at Union Carbide if foreigners buy it?

No matter who owns any company, unless the government subsidizes it, it can succeed only by giving its customers what they need and want. When a company does so, it doesn't matter who owns it.

The Future

If you aren't alarmed by the thought of all those foreigners owning American stocks, bonds, and real estate, there's more to the story.

A study by the Congressional Research Service showed that—if the trend continues unchanged—the net U.S. foreign debt (which was claimed to be $368 billion at the end of 1987) would rise to $1 *trillion* by 1991, and over $2 trillion in 1995. The 1995 figure is one fourth of the projected U.S. Gross National Product for 1995.[2]

Straight-line forecasts of this kind—projecting the latest yearly changes out into the future—always predict something worrisome and bizarre. In January you can say with perfect accuracy that if the current weather continues, Chicago will be buried under 300 feet of snow by August.

The Object

Suppose the debt figures really were debt figures—not stocks, real estate, and so forth. And suppose we really did owe more than is owed to us—with more being paid in interest and dividends than is being received.

If those things *were* true, the burning question would be "So what?" What are we supposed to do about it?

---

[2]Reported in the *San Francisco Examiner,* July 4, 1988. Realize that this study, too, was confusing debt with stocks and other assets.

Encourage each American to lend money to a German?

Burn down all factories owned by foreigners?

Subsidize every American who opens a Swiss bank account?

Start a War Bond drive—to get Americans to buy Iranian War Bonds?

No, of course not. But the absurdity of the solutions demonstrates the absurdity of the "problem"—the idea that it's dangerous for America to become so attractive that people from all over the world want to invest here.

But don't misunderstand me. The "debtor nation" label isn't a merit badge either. The whole matter is mostly a statistical curiosity (like the number of years the Boston Celtics won the NBA basketball championship). It has real importance only to a few people (such as those who live in Boston), but it doesn't have the slightest effect on the well-being of anyone else.

The purpose of the "selling of America" story (and the reason some people love it) is to show that the low-tax policies of the 1980s were foolish and must be reversed. Dear Lord, send us a tax increase to balance the budget, end the need for the government to borrow abroad, stop this orgy of consumption, and make America a creditor nation once again.

If America falls for this approach, our chains will be a little tighter, and the time bomb will go off a little sooner. But ten years from today I'm sure our "debt" position will be just as alarming.

We'll seem even deeper in bondage to the Albanians or Costa Ricans—or whoever are the 1990s' equivalent of the Arabs in the 1970s and the Japanese in the 1980s.

10

Avoiding the Crises

T here is no end to the non-problems that the government may invite itself to solve. The four I've discussed—the government's supposed lack of revenue, the stock market crash, the trade deficit, and the presumed disgrace of being a debtor nation—are only examples. More are surely on the way.

You may be able to recognize them when they arrive in news reports and political speeches. A non-problem has a familiar profile to it.

First, statistics are usually cited to prove that the problem exists. But you won't be given a chance to examine the statistics closely, nor will you be told very much about how the statistical evidence was compiled or why someone went to all the trouble in the first place.

The "debtor nation" scandal is a good example. Rarely is the size of the "debt" mentioned. Even rarer is any explanation of how the figures were compiled or what was counted. And we've never been told who ran around Europe appraising the villas owned by Americans.[1]

[1]Maybe it was Robin Leach.

Second, even if the problem happens to have a little substance, it will be framed in such a way that one obvious solution follows from it as night follows the day. No other solution will be discussed, except with a sneer, even if it might solve the problem with smaller costs and fewer side effects.

For example, if the issue is the trade deficit, it will be framed as an excess of imports—not as a shortfall of exports. The obvious remedy for the glut of imports will be to shut the door on foreign products. That this will also shut the door on American consumers won't be mentioned; nor will much be said of the idea that lower taxes could make American exports more competitive, except to dismiss it as another handout for the rich.

Third, the one obvious solution will require an expansion of the government's size, scope, and powers. Either the government must spend more money, or the government must stop people from doing something, or the government must compel them to do something. Whatever the problem, the proposed solution will add to the enormous burden of government that the economy is already carrying.

And you can be doubly certain that the solution won't call for the government to get out of the way. If the discussion is about the homeless, you won't hear a demand that rent-control laws be repealed to encourage the construction of more housing. Or if it's claimed that there's a lack of affordable child-care facilities, the options won't include judicial reform to limit the power of courts to bankrupt small companies through extravagant liability judgments.

Or if you're told to worry that the gap between rich and poor is widening, no one will mention that the poor who aren't getting richer are mainly the government's permanent welfare clients.

Finally, the proposed solution will be presented as beneficial for all of us—except for a few villains, who will get what they deserve.

There will be no attempt to trace all the potential consequences and side effects. If it's a plan to tighten the screws on South Africa, the promoters won't notice (until it's too late) that a number of strategic metals—such as platinum and chromium—are available virtually only from South Africa and the Soviet Union.[2]

When someone wants to force every U.S. company to provide medical insurance for its employees, he won't wonder aloud how the employers can pay the bill—or whether their only option will be to reduce wages. Nor will he consider the possibility that forced spending for health care will push up the prices paid for medical care by people who don't have any insurance.

These characteristics of non-problems are hints that a desired solution motivated a search for a suitable problem—not the reverse, as you might have expected.

GOVERNMENT

By now, you may be getting the impression that I'm not very fond of government programs.

You're right.

I don't worry about the follies of anyone but the government. It wouldn't alarm me if General Motors chose to double its prices. Or if the United Mine Workers decided to strike for double wages. Neither GM nor the UMW can hurt the economy without hurting itself much more.

No private company or group of workers can force anyone to pay its price. Nor can it keep competitors from rushing in to fill the void when it behaves foolishly—whether by charging too much or by giving too little in return.

Only the government can be the fool that everyone must bear— whose losses we all must pay.

Only the government can create a shortage and then prevent competition from solving it—whether the shortage is of oil, education, prompt mail service, water, electricity, or anything else. Critical shortages—those that become national issues—are

[2]*Commodity Yearbook 1988,* Commodity Research Bureau, pages 31 and 190.

always caused (1) by government taking over an industry and forbidding competition (as with postal service); or (2) by government outlawing competition, appointing a single supplier, and regulating it to death (as with electric and water utilities); or (3) by government imposing price controls on producers (as with oil in the 1970s). No private entity has such power to disrupt the economy.

Only government can run up debts endlessly without fear of foreclosure—because only government can print however many dollars are required to pay its creditors. So only government can create interest rates high enough to paralyze the economy.

Only government can create inflation—by printing too many of the dollars with which we measure the prices of things.

Only government can tie up the economy in a straitjacket of regulation.

Misdirection

I mention these things because it's easy to look the wrong way when you're watching for a crisis.

Every crisis book or article I've seen in the past few years claimed or implied that our problems were caused by government doing too little—not too much. But that's the philosophy that created our troubles. Governments cause problems, the problems become noticeable, the proposed solutions lead to more government, the problems grow, the solutions become more drastic, and eventually the problems escalate into crises.

We have nothing to fear from inside traders, the rich getting richer, people spending their money as they want, Americans incurring debts as they choose and as their creditors allow, or poorly managed companies that try to succeed without satisfying their customers.

If the 1990s are a decade of crises, it will be because too many people have expected the government to solve every problem, grant every wish, satisfy every grievance, and resolve every dispute.[3]

It will be because two generations of Americans have grown up with virtually no notion of how wealth is produced—since they've been nurtured with the belief that government can make us all wealthy just by snapping its federal fingers.

It will be because those who wield the power of government are bound to abuse it sooner or later—and we've finally arrived at "later."

Averting the Crises

Can the crises be averted?

Yes, it's possible. But it isn't likely.

AVOIDING THE MONETARY CRISIS

To avoid the monetary crisis, the Federal Reserve would have to return *very soon* to the 1978–82 policy of stable money growth.

Doing so would be painful, since the chaotic money growth of 1982–88 has already made a recession almost inevitable. But the alternative is a decade or more of pain as the economy is tossed back and forth between inflation and recession.

Long-term Solutions

But even if the Fed did seem to return to a stable policy this year, how soon would it fall off the wagon again? Would next year's Federal Reserve governors be as adamant about a stable monetary

---

[3]In the recent election campaign, did you hear any candidate answer a "What will you do about . . ." question by saying, "Nothing—that isn't a matter for government to handle." I left my porch light on every night, hoping that a presidential candidate would come to my door. I wanted to ask what he planned to do about the shortage of neo-classical operetta in America.

policy? Or would they crank up the money machine to try to end the recession quickly?

Stability will be temporary so long as the supply of money is controlled by the government. Only when money is created naturally, through the operation of the marketplace or by an impersonal gold standard, will we be free of the uncertainty and instability that are generated by the Federal Reserve's discretionary power.

Will the Federal Reserve keep us off the inflation-recession seesaw in the 1990s?

It's possible, but very unlikely.

AVOIDING THE DEBT CRISIS

Is it possible that the federal deficits can be eliminated before they send interest rates soaring?

Yes, it's possible, but three conditions are required:

1. Government spending must be frozen long enough for revenues to catch up. As we saw in Chapter 6, any tax increase that seems large enough to close the deficit would be large enough to devastate the economy.
2. A spending freeze requires that no program be allowed to increase automatically. Otherwise, the next recession will send government spending soaring.
3. Balancing the current budget isn't enough. With the present level of federal debt, we've survived only because interest rates have been falling and the economy has been healthy. If interest rates rise—for any reason—the refinancing of existing debt could demolish the credit markets. We can escape this danger permanently only by reducing the federal debt through many years of budget surpluses.

These three conditions are a lot to expect from the same public servants who created the problem. But anything less would leave us permanently vulnerable to a debt crisis—even if we were able to elude one for now.

AVOIDING THE BANKING CRISIS

The news about banks is a little brighter.

Most bankers realize how vulnerable they've become. Over the past few years, banks have been cleaning house in two ways.

First, they've faced up to the poor quality of their outstanding loans and increased their reserves for potential loan losses. Large banks have acknowledged and adjusted to the fact that many of their loans to foreign governments may never be repaid.

Second, banks aren't so cavalier about mismatching maturities as they used to be. For example, they are emphasizing adjustable-rate mortgages—a practice that protects banks during periods of rising interest rates.

But banks in general still are dangerously illiquid. So they continue to be vulnerable to anything that encourages depositors to avoid using banks. They can survive only so long as the credibility of the FDIC sticker survives.

That's a slender reed upon which to rest the weight of the entire banking system.

Regulation

The deregulation of FDIC-insured banks in the 1980s has left them in no-man's-land. They now have greater freedom to take risks with depositors' money—and they can still send the bill to the FDIC if something goes wrong.

Needless to say, the cries from the critics are for more government—to re-regulate the banks. But banking problems have been growing for decades, since long before deregulation got under way in the late 1970s. It's true, however, that the problems have accelerated since deregulation.

With or without regulation, most banks will be either weak or wild so long as they're sheltered by the FDIC. If the FDIC were dissolved and all regulation removed, the banks would compete in the same free market as other companies. With no

FDIC to bail them out, depositors would move money from the weaker banks to the stronger ones. Banks would have to behave more cautiously, and find ways to prove to customers that their deposits were safe.

Back to the Present

But this really is idle musing. We've come a long way in the 1980s toward trusting consumers to take care of themselves, but I doubt that any plan to give consumers sovereignty over the banking industry is stirring in the breast of the new president.

For now, the banking crisis can be averted only if most banks reform themselves before they're hit by the next interest-rate shock. Obviously, not all banks will become liquid enough, no matter how much time they're given.

Under any circumstances, the savings & loan industry probably is already past saving. As the news about the savings & loans gets worse and worse, too many people will try to transfer their money from savings & loan associations to banks. That will bring down almost all associations—even those that are solvent but illiquid. Ten years from now, savings & loans might be merely a history-book curiosity.

Because many people think banks are different from savings & loans, the run on savings & loans might not spread to banks and credit unions. But we won't know until the time comes.

INTERDEPENDENCE

A further cause for pessimism today is the extent to which each of the problems can affect the others.

An interest-rate crisis brought on by the federal deficit would turn existing bank loans into money-losers, and push the economy into a recession.

A recession would not only be painful in itself, but would magnify the federal deficit and multiply loan losses at banks.

And if confidence in the banking system evaporates, the first response from the government might be a budget-busting handout from Congress to the FDIC—and the Federal Reserve could wind up printing enough money to guarantee galloping inflation.

Each problem is dangerous enough by itself. But a blow-up for any one of the three would be only the first in a string of explosions.

TIMING

The economic time bomb is only a metaphor; we can't look at its clock to see how much time is left. A crisis could erupt tomorrow morning—or next month—or next year—or possibly even several years from now.

It may be tempting to hope that we have a few years left—in which case arranging protection for yourself wouldn't be so urgent. I hope you'll resist that temptation.

Or you might hesitate to arrange protection because you imagine that it would be expensive—in terms of your time and attention, the investment profits that must be forgone, and the "fortress mentality" you'd have to adopt.

I'm happy to inform you that safety can be inexpensive. Your investment in knowledge will cost only about three hours—the time it takes to read Part II.

And once you've done that, you may decide—as I have—that proper protection is really rather simple and painless.

It won't increase your risks; it should reduce them. It doesn't require that you become a sophisticated speculator; it accepts you as you are now. It won't ask for a great deal of time to carry out the plan; a couple of days should be enough. It doesn't call for vigilance; one day a year to monitor your portfolio should be plenty.

And it doesn't mean forgoing good times. You can continue to live a normal life and continue to seek profits.

PART II

Protection & Profit
in an
Uncertain World

11

Dealing with Uncertainty

Part II presents an investment program that can take care of you for the decade to come—no matter how troubled or serene the decade turns out to be.

We'll begin by looking at seven principles that any successful investment program must respect. None of these principles is very surprising. What is surprising is how often prudent, sensible individuals get hurt by neglecting them.

REALITY VS. FANTASY

Principle #1: *Look at investing in the same way you view the rest of your life.*

The rules of life that have brought you to where you are today shouldn't be forgotten or forsaken when you think about investing. Reality in the investment world is the same as it is in your professional life, in family life, or in any other endeavor.

For example, investment forecasts can be exciting. But in any other area of life, we call people who claim to predict the future *fortune-tellers*—and we think of them as entertainers.

It may be intriguing to read that "the stock market is in its third upward wave and will have an important top on the 15th of next month." But in other areas of life, we call people who talk that way *crackpots*—and we'd never dream of betting precious capital on their mysterious insights.

It can be fascinating to hear someone explain how the graph of an investment's price reveals a "head-and-shoulders pattern" that foretells a major change in direction. But elsewhere in life, we think of people who see the future in lines and squiggles as superstitious—and we pride ourselves that our lives aren't directed by old wives' tales.

Somehow, when the subject is money, most people are fair game for *any* idea—even if it violates the realism and clear thinking that have brought about their business and personal success.

It even seems that the more mystical or fantastic the idea, the more likely investors are to fall for it. When the subject is investing, skepticism is forgotten, and we rush eagerly into the Twilight Zone.

PREDICTIONS

Principle #2: *No one can predict the future.*

The world of economics and investments revolves around forecasts. Economists, investment advisors, and brokers continually draw upon their knowledge and expertise to tell us what's coming next.

And each one is right occasionally—which gives him something to boast about for the rest of his career. But no one can predict the future in a consistent and profitable way. In two decades in the investment business, I haven't come across a single soul who could reliably foretell next year's interest rates, gold price, inflation rate, or stock-market results.

I have, however, come across many, many people who *claim* to be consistently correct in their predictions. Some of them have impressive endorsements from impartial observers who say they've verified a forecaster's claims. But once I begin keeping track of the forecaster's predictions, he somehow loses his touch. He still manages to see the future correctly now and then—but no more often than my barber.

Human Action

Why would we expect anyone to be able to predict economic events and investment prices?

Investment prices reflect the ideas and actions of millions of human beings. The price of a stock or the volume of borrowing or the supply of wheat each results from decisions that human beings have made and acted upon—human beings all over the world.

These people are complicated, inscrutable creatures. Their actions spring from an assortment of experiences, beliefs, and emotions. How presumptuous it is to think that I can sort through that jumble to foresee the result flowing from the many intricate and opposing forces at work.

Some forecasters bypass the complications by saying that everything moves by predictable mass psychology—as though mass psychology will determine the credit needs of a businessman, the planting requirements of a farmer, or the political choices of a Federal Reserve governor—and as though everyone else were a robot, but you and I had free will.

The complexities of human action are often dismissed with the slogan "Human nature never changes." But humans are always learning, always changing as they acquire new information—so that the most striking characteristic of human action is its unpredictability. The study of history can teach us what is possible, but it can't show us what must happen.

If someone can predict human action, he should be able to predict sporting events and make a fortune betting on them. If he can predict economic events, he can make a new fortune every year by warning companies about the plans and future actions of competitors.

And if someone could predict investment prices profitably, he could own half the world within a decade or two. So you aren't likely to find him wasting his time in a brokerage office, writing books or newsletters, or advising politicians.

Predictions are especially unreliable when they concern crises. How can anyone know which particular straw will break the hartebeest's back?

What Everyone Knows

Some events seem inevitable because history appears to be rushing headlong in one direction. But "sure things" are the most dangerous bets of all.

In April 1980 the inflation rate was 15% and had been rising steadily since 1976. Books, articles, and brokerage reports were agreed on one thing: inflation was here to stay. The only question was how high it would go.

But within two years inflation was cut in half, and in three years it had virtually disappeared.

The biggest losers in the prosperous economy of the 1980s were the people who had bet heavily that inflation would continue— bets they placed by buying real estate, farms, gold, and other commodities with loans they intended to repay someday with "cheaper dollars."

Why We Look at the Future

By all means, peer into the future. But do it to *imagine* what others are overlooking—to discover possibilities you might have ignored—to see whether something might be emerging that your plans haven't allowed for—to be aware of what could go wrong. Whatever you see, remember that it's your imagination that sees it—not your eyes.

If you fool yourself into believing you *know* what's ahead, you're playing Russian Roulette. A single mistake could be fatal to your wealth.

FALLIBILITY

Principle #3: *No one can get you into and out of investments consistently with precise and profitable timing.*

We've all heard, at some time or other, about a wizard who foresees all the major moves in the investment markets. This legendary genius has made fortunes for people you know, or for people known by people you know, or for people known by people known by people you've shaken hands with.

But, somehow, *you've* never been privy to the wisdom and inside knowledge of a financial genius. You've never experienced the excitement and profit of getting into an investment on the ground floor and riding it all the way to the top—selling out just before the price plunges.

The reason you haven't found such a person is simple: he doesn't exist. Better to search for the Wizard of Oz than for the Wizard of Wall Street.

Jumping on the Bandwagon

I don't mean that no one ever has a lucky streak. We all do.

Sometimes a broker, writer, or advisor makes several profitable recommendations in a row. But you didn't act on his advice, because you hadn't even heard of him. Only *after* he's compiled his winning streak—and *because* of it—do you become aware of him. By then his lucky streak is running out, and he's ready to begin losing—the day you start acting on his advice.

The Hulbert Financial Digest monitors the model portfolios of over 100 popular investment newsletters, noting every recommendation, to determine how profitable the advisor's advice has been. Each issue names the newsletters with the best recent results. But the names keep changing; last year's genius never seems to be in the news this year.

Of course, we know we're supposed to pay attention only to *long-term* performance records. But the lists of long-term winners are just as variable. The newsletter with the best record for the latest 5-year period might not even make the top 10 of next year's 5-year list. And, at any one time, the lists of advisors with the best 5-year, 6-year, and 7-year records differ considerably from each other.

Falling Off the Bandwagon

The newsletter with the best 7-year record through June 30, 1987, had compiled a gain of exactly 600%—which is a compound profit of 32% per year. Now that's genius. But if you started acting on this newsletter's recommendations on October 1, 1987, you would have lost 57% of your capital *in one month.*

Of course, even after that disastrous month, the newsletter was still 200% ahead since 1980. But that was irrelevant to nearly all of its readers. Hardly anyone had followed the newsletter's advice continuously since 1980, because hardly anyone knew it existed in 1980. Only *after* the winning record was compiled did the newsletter become known and investors begin acting on its advice.

Another newsletter had the #1 profit records for both 1985 and 1986, but lost 58% when the stock market crashed in October 1987.

Why do these reversals happen? Because spectacular winning streaks come more from luck than from talent. Out of thousands of investment advisors, mere chance dictates that a few of them will be riding lucky streaks on any day. But the only sure thing about luck is that it changes eventually. When an investment advisor's luck is good, he becomes a celebrity, he attracts a crowd of new clients, and then his luck turns bad.[1]

The situation is the same for mutual funds. Last year's big winners rarely repeat their successes this year. For the final calendar quarter of 1985, Strategic Capital Gains had the best performance record of the 973 funds monitored by Lipper Analytical Services. The very next quarter, the fund finished 973rd—dead last.[2]

TRADING SYSTEMS

Principle #4: *No trading system or market indicator will get you into and out of investments profitably over a period of time.*

Trading systems (methods for determining when to buy and sell investments) are like advisors: they all have wonderful performance records, but they never come through when *your* money is on the line.

I know of no investment advisor who is currently promoting the same trading system he was selling 5 years ago. Advisors continually overhaul or replace their systems—which is a strong sign that the systems don't work. Be warned that the system to which you commit yourself today probably will be discarded by its creator tomorrow.

OVERINVESTING IN ONE PLACE

Principle #5: *Don't keep all your capital in one kind of investment.*

If you keep your money all in bank CDs, or all in gold, or all in stocks, you're vulnerable to sudden, devastating losses that can be caused by a single event.

[1]The performance information is taken from *The Hulbert Financial Digest* (316 Commerce Street, Alexandria, Virginia 22314; $135 per year, $25 for a sample issue), July 27, 1987, and November 30, 1987, issues.
[2]*Barron's*, May 19, 1986, page 47.

Every investment gets battered sooner or later. Stocks lost 35% of their value between August and October of 1987. And they were a poor investment for most of the 1970s. Bonds and bank accounts were ravaged by inflation in the 1970s. And gold, which rose 20 times over in the 1970s, has lost half of its value so far in the 1980s.

But it's also true that every investment has its day in the sun. So a permanent *combination* of investments, if carefully chosen, can flourish in all economic climates.

INVESTING VS. SPECULATING

Principle #6: *Recognize the difference between investing and speculating.*

Investors accept whatever rate of return the investment markets are providing, while they protect what they have—protect it from depreciation, confiscation, inflation, or anything else that might rob them.

Speculators risk what they have in an attempt to *beat* the markets—to outguess them—to win big by being in the right place at the right time.

If you had most of your money in blue-chip stocks in October 1987, you may have thought you were investing. But by concentrating your capital in one place, you were speculating—guessing that stocks would continue to be the leading investment. And you paid dearly for having guessed wrong.

You're speculating whenever you bet everything you have on one investment, on your ability to get out when the investment peaks, or on your belief that you know more than other investors. You're speculating—even if someone assures you that you're making a conservative investment.

There's nothing wrong with speculating—*provided you do it with money you can afford to lose.*

THE DREAM WORLD

We can sum up with **Principle #7:** *In the world of economics and investments, almost nothing turns out as expected.*

Forecasts rarely come true. Trading systems never produce the results advertised for them. Investment advisors and brokers with records of phenomenal success somehow run into losing streaks when *you* start acting on their advice. The most careful and logical analysis of an investment or the economy usually proves later to have overlooked the most significant event.

Investors, advisors, and economists love to talk about the forces that are leading inevitably to one thing or another. They talk about the fundamentals, the technical aspects, the cyclical movements, the historical forces, the political pressures, the unfolding economic future. But all the talk is simply that—talk. Rarely does anything unfold in the way it was expected to.

And yet most investors continue to plan and act as though the future were entirely predictable—as though the right investment advisor or system could lead them into and out of investments with precise, profitable timing—as though some indicator or other device could tell them what an investment will do next.

Why do investors keep placing their faith in talk that never produces anything? Because their eyes are so glued on the future that they don't look back to see that nothing before turned out as it was supposed to.

If you take predictions seriously, no single forecast holds your attention for very long. You don't ignore everything else until the forecast proves to have been right or wrong. Before the forecast has been verified or disproven by events, your attention is diverted by new forecasts. And because you're preoccupied with forecasts for next year, you won't check back to see how badly the forecasts for this year turned out.

You can approach investing realistically only if you realize that almost nothing turns out as expected.

LIVING WITH THE TIME BOMB

The economic time bomb may explode one day soon, with grave consequences.

But I can't predict the future—any more than anyone else can. I can only survey the present and try to see what *could* come next. Part I wasn't a road map or a timetable. It was a plea that you take the dangers seriously.

Because I think the crises are so likely, and because I believe they may be severe, the time has come to speak up. I want you to be protected from whatever might happen.

But you won't be protecting yourself if you bet everything you have on one possible outcome, or on the trading advice of any investment guru. That's as dangerous as doing nothing.

You need a program for protection that frees you from having to wonder which of the possibilities raised in Part I will come to pass—or how or when they'll occur.

Fortunately, there's a way to protect yourself without foreseeing the future—and without forsaking the chance to profit if, somehow, the problems don't run out of control.

How to do that is the subject of Part II.

12

A Strategy for
Safety & Profit

To protect you against the unknown, your investment strategy must satisfy six requirements:

1. The investments you hold must do well in any economic climate—inflation, recession, prosperity, or anything else.
2. Your strategy must require *no* forecasting. Forecasts are not only unreliable, they're dangerous. One wrong forecast could wipe you out. No matter how confident anyone may be about the shape of the future, your financial security shouldn't depend on the success of a forecast.
3. Your investment program should *not* have to change as the economic climate and investment trends change. You can't be certain whether today's trend will end tomorrow or will continue for years. Any opinion about trends is a forecast; acting on the opinion is a speculation.
4. Your investment program must be able to withstand *all* surprises—including events that will be as unexpected as the government's confiscation of gold in 1933, the imposition of wage and price controls in 1971, the devaluations of the

dollar in 1971 and 1973, the collapse of inflation in 1980, and the stock market crash in 1987.

5. The strategy must allow you to "walk away" from your investments—to forget about them, if you like—confident that, whatever happens, your investments are taking care of you. Otherwise you'll never be able to think about anything but investments.

6. If you have a strong opinion about the future, the strategy must leave room for you to bet on that opinion without endangering the capital that's precious to you.

THE PERMANENT PORTFOLIO

The first five objectives require investments that allow for anything the future might hold. But what investment can do that?

No single investment can. But the right *combination* of investments has the power to take care of you in any situation.

You shouldn't judge an investment in isolation, as though it might be the only thing you will own. Safety won't be found in a single investment that is right for all seasons—because no such investment exists. And you won't find security by trying to jump from one investment to another as the seasons change. Safety is reached only with a *group* of investments that is so well balanced it can protect you in all circumstances—without ever being altered.

Such a group must be assembled carefully. Just throwing together this and that won't bring you balance and safety—even if you pile up dozens of different investments. Each element of the portfolio must serve a definite purpose—to take care of you in a specific economic situation. When its time comes, each investment must be powerful enough to pull the entire portfolio upward—even if all the other investments are suffering.

A combination of investments that will do all this is called a

Permanent Portfolio, because—once established—the portfolio *is* permanent. You don't tinker with it whenever the economic outlook seems to be changing. You leave it alone—to hold the same investments, in the same proportions, permanently.

The primary purpose of the Permanent Portfolio is to preserve your capital, no matter what the future brings. But, if it's properly constructed, the Permanent Portfolio also should enjoy reasonable growth in almost any economic climate—prosperity, inflation, or recession.

For the Permanent Portfolio to work, you must be willing to leave it alone to do its job—no matter how excited you become about an investment opportunity. Once you start speculating with the Permanent Portfolio, it loses its ability to protect you from the surprises that the future has in store for you.

THE VARIABLE PORTFOLIO

There's nothing wrong with speculating—but do it *outside* the Permanent Portfolio, with money you are willing to risk losing. Create a second portfolio that does nothing but speculate, so that safety and speculation are never confused.

The second portfolio is called the Variable Portfolio—because you vary its investments as your judgment dictates.

With a Variable Portfolio, you can bet on anything at any time. You might buy a selection of stocks when you believe a new bull market is starting—or you might limit your money to, say, computer stocks if you expect them to lead the pack. You might buy gold when you think inflation is about to heat up—or bonds if you think interest rates are about to fall.

You might buy platinum if you think that U.S. sanctions will reduce the supply of platinum from South Africa. Or you might simply hold cash while you wait for an attractive opportunity.

An investment for the Variable Portfolio might be a quickie—

such as a commodity futures contract that will last only a few days. Or you might buy stocks or real estate that you expect to hold profitably for several years.

Freedom to Speculate

The Variable Portfolio should be funded with money you can afford to lose, so that no loss can damage your standard of living or destroy your security.

When you're speculating only with risk capital, you don't have to be concerned about safety. So your decisions for the Variable Portfolio can depend solely on your current outlook for investments.

With the Variable Portfolio, you can make any speculation you choose. If your timing is wrong or some surprise sends history off in an unforeseen direction, your Permanent Portfolio is still there to protect you—unhurt by the speculation that didn't work out.

And by giving you the freedom to speculate, the Variable Portfolio makes it easier for you to keep your hands off the Permanent Portfolio.

DIVIDING YOUR CAPITAL

How much of your capital should go into the Variable Portfolio?

The maximum limit is whatever capital you can afford to lose. If you're cautious with the Variable Portfolio, you probably won't lose all the money—even if every speculation turns out badly. But you must be sure that none of the money with which you speculate is precious to you.

Of the amount you decide you can risk, the specific sum you allocate to the Variable Portfolio should reflect how adventurous you are and how much interest you have in speculating. If you have no interest in betting on the future, or if you have no capital you can afford to lose, you shouldn't have a Variable Portfolio at all.

If you're going to have a Variable Portfolio, you must decide how much to put into it at the time you set up your overall investment plan—before you make your first speculation. If you try to make the decision when you're excited by a specific opportunity, you can easily overestimate the amount you'd be willing to lose.

TWO PORTFOLIOS

A Permanent Portfolio, properly arranged, offers the best security possible. No one's ability to divine the future is nearly as reliable. The Permanent Portfolio will take care of you in *any* situation— not just when you're at your best or your luck is good.

If you believe you can see what's coming ahead of time, if you think your foresight and talent can produce big profits, by all means bet on your expectations for the future—with money you've set aside for that purpose in a Variable Portfolio.

If you aren't interested in betting on investment trends, if you always try to avoid the people who talk about investments at cocktail parties, don't bother with a Variable Portfolio.

But if you're ever likely to get an itch to bet on the future, you should have a Variable Portfolio with which to scratch it—even if you can afford only $1,000 for it. Otherwise, you'll find yourself tampering with the Permanent Portfolio, and your program for safety will start to come apart.

If you're a good speculator, and if your luck is good, the Variable Portfolio may make you rich. But it serves an even more important purpose: it's a safety valve that allows you to act on your impulses without putting the Permanent Portfolio in danger.

The next five chapters will explain how the Permanent Portfolio achieves the ambitious goals I've set for it. And Chapter 18 will discuss the Variable Portfolio further.

Once the Permanent Portfolio is in position, you'll be safe from the economic time bomb. You won't need to change your investments every time you hear a new horror story on the evening news.

13

A Simple Plan for Complete Protection

The Permanent Portfolio's first job is to keep your capital safe in all circumstances. It must be sturdy enough to withstand the economic time bomb—which means it must be able to survive a monetary crisis, a debt crisis, or a banking crisis.

But that isn't enough. The Permanent Portfolio must be ready for *any* crisis. You need to know you'll be safe in any economic climate—including events and circumstances that neither you nor I have imagined. And the portfolio should let you profit while prosperity continues—even if the prosperity of the 1980s continues right on through the 1990s.

That may sound like a tall order, but there's a practical way for you to fill it.

Although there are millions of possibilities for the future, you don't need to worry about all of them. Most of what happens in the economy and the investment markets is just static, with no long-term significance. Stocks are up one day and back down the next; inflation goes up a little one month and then levels off.

149

You don't need to be concerned with every twitch in the economy or every little flutter in the investment markets, because your portfolio doesn't have to profit every single day—or even every month.

It *is* important that your portfolio be able to react well to every broad movement in the economy. And these broad movements fit into four general economic situations:

1. *Prosperity:* A period in which living standards are rising, the economy is growing, business is thriving, and unemployment is declining.
2. *Inflation:* A period when consumer prices in general are rising. They might be rising slowly (an inflation rate of 5% or so), rapidly (10% to 20% or so), or at a runaway rate (25% or more).
3. *Tight money:* A period during which the money supply is shrinking or its growth rate is slowing. This leaves people with less cash than they expected to have. Tight money often leads to a recession—a period of poor economic conditions. Continued long enough, tight money will lead to deflation and depression.
4. *Deflation:* The opposite of inflation. Consumer prices decline, and the purchasing power of money grows. Deflation often has been accompanied by depression—a prolonged period of very bad economic conditions. The last significant deflation in America was during 1929–33.[1]

The four economic environments frequently overlap. Inflation often is rising toward the end of a period of prosperity, for example. And inflation usually doesn't start declining until after many months of tight money.

But these four conditions are all-inclusive; at any time, one of them will predominate. So if your Permanent Portfolio is ready for all four of them, it's ready for anything.

---

[1]*Disinflation,* in contrast to deflation, is a fall in the inflation rate. Consumer prices are still rising, but they're rising more slowly than they were before. The period of 1980–86 was one of disinflation, as the inflation rate fell from 15% to 1%.

Other Events

Investments are affected by events arising outside the financial system. War, changes in government intervention, civil turmoil, and elections all affect investment prices. But if they have a long-term impact on investments, it is by pushing the economy from one to another of the four environments.

ELEMENTS OF THE PORTFOLIO

No single investment does well in all economic climates. So the Permanent Portfolio must prosper by combining different elements—each of which responds well in one or more of the four circumstances.

Prosperity

To begin with, you'll need an investment that profits from prosperity. We don't know how long it will be before the economic time bomb goes off. Prosperity might continue for a number of years. And even when the economy is finally overwhelmed by the crises, we won't know just how long it will take to recover.

The obvious choice for an investment that profits from prosperity is common stocks.

Stocks usually begin to do well as a recession approaches its end. They might rise from depressed levels because the economy is recovering naturally from a recession. Or it may be that the stock market is benefiting from the new money the government has been printing to fight the recession.

In either case, stocks continue to appreciate as prosperity expands. If money growth is relatively stable, the bull market may last for several years.

But if the prosperity is due to rapid money growth, inflation will follow. And eventually, that will force the government to switch to a tight-money policy that will choke off the bull market.

Inflation

Inflation is still dormant today, compared to the 1970s. But the Federal Reserve may soon find itself creating new money at a furious pace—to cure the next recession, to finance the government's borrowing needs, or to buy time for sick banks.

Gold is the best investment for protection from inflation. Most things rise in price during an inflation, but gold's response is the most reliable and the most powerful.

Unlike other commodities, gold is primarily a monetary metal. Its principal function is as a store of value—a role in which it competes with the U.S. dollar. The demand for gold grows when rising inflation casts doubt on the dollar's future purchasing power. Thus gold's performance is tied directly to inflation—rather than being an incidental consequence of it.

Because the existing stockpile of gold held by investors all over the world is so large, the comparatively small levels of mine production and industrial consumption have an insignificant effect on the price of gold. Demand for gold as a store of value dominates the price. Thus gold's response to inflation is much more powerful and reliable than that of commodities whose prices are determined by levels of production and consumption.

Gold also has the virtue of being self-sufficient. Unlike most investments, it isn't a piece of paper that promises to do something or deliver something at a later date. You can hold gold in your hand. This self-sufficiency means that gold, unlike other inflation hedges, can do its job even if the financial markets break down. Gold can respond just as effectively to the chaos of runaway inflation as it does to the inconvenience of mild inflation.

Gold also may profit from political or military crises that feed anxiety and increase the demand for a store of value. During periods of declining inflation (such as the mid-1980s), crises that cause the demand for money to rise are bullish for the U.S. dollar. But during periods of rising inflation (such as the late 1970s), such events increase the demand for gold. So if a political or military crisis occurs during an inflationary period, gold can profit from it.

Tight Money

Periods of tight money occur when the Federal Reserve, worried about inflation, significantly slows the growth of the money supply.

If the slow money growth continues for 6 months to a year or more, it probably will bring on a recession—a period when the economy is faltering, many companies are in trouble, and unemployment is spreading.

Periods of tight money often begin while gold is still in a bull market. Gold may continue to rise for a while, because it takes time for changes in money growth to affect inflation. But eventually, tight money is sure to kill off a bull market in gold.

And by curtailing the supply of credit, tight money pushes interest rates upward—which causes bond prices to go down. Tight money also drains liquidity and value out of the stock market. Sooner or later, tight money forces *all* investments downward.

The portfolio's surest protection against tight money is in cash-like investments—such as Treasury bills or other short-term securities that promise to repay a fixed number of dollars. Because cash doesn't fluctuate in price, it moderates any decline in a portfolio's overall value. And the interest earned by the cash will further soften the blow—especially since interest rates tend to be high during periods of tight money.

But even with part of the portfolio in cash, a period of tight money won't be profitable for a Permanent Portfolio. As a rule, the interest earned won't completely overcome the losses in other investments.

However, the perverse effect of tight money is inherently self-limiting. Unlike prosperity or inflation, it can't go on indefinitely; it is only a transition to something else.

The economy may adjust to the lower rate of money growth after a while, and a new bull market in stocks will begin. Or the Federal Reserve may relent and step up monetary growth—causing stocks, and possibly gold, to boom. Or the Fed may persist with tight money too long—bringing on a deflation and big profits in bonds.

Deflation

Anytime the Federal Reserve tries to squeeze inflation out of the economy by slowing money growth, it runs the risk of squeezing too hard. If tight money continues long enough, it will lead to deflation—and a full-blown depression. The inflation rate would fall to low levels, then to zero—and then consumer prices would start to decline.

Stocks would continue to lose value because the companies they represent would be losing money. Gold would be hurt because the dollar would be becoming more valuable—not less, as during inflation.

Cash would help the portfolio during a deflation, because its purchasing power would grow. And the interest it earned would be a further bonus.

But the biggest winner should be the very highest-grade bonds. With dollars becoming more valuable, interest rates would fall eventually to very low levels—perhaps 2% to 3%. As interest rates fell, bond prices would rise.

During the Depression of the 1930s, for example, the interest yield on U.S. Treasury bonds fell to 2%. Such a yield in the 1990s would push the prices of 25-year bonds to three or four times their 1988 levels.

At the very beginning of the depression, bonds—like other investments—might still be suffering the effects of tight money. But having bonds in the portfolio assures that at least one investment would have a significant gain at some point during the difficult times.

Bonds also help the portfolio any other time interest rates fall. During 1981–86, for example, when the yield on U.S. Treasury bonds fell from 15% to 7½%, most long-term bonds doubled in price.

Full Coverage

Surprisingly, just four investments—stocks, gold, bonds, and cash—provide coverage for all the broad economic possibilities.

They do so because, unlike most investments, each of them is moved almost entirely by the general direction of the economy—rather than by weather conditions, changes in consumer tastes, or technological innovations.[2]

NEUTRALITY OR GROWTH?

It might seem that a portfolio containing opposing investments would be neutralized: as one element rose, another would go down—and nothing would be gained.

On a day-to-day basis, that's often true. But over broad periods of time, the winning investments tend to add more value to the portfolio than the losing investments take away.

For example, 1973–77 was a poor time for stocks. The New York Stock Exchange Index fell 20% (from 65 to 52). But gold

[2]Individual stocks are affected by changes in taste and technology. But the individual differences are averaged out in a diversified group of stocks that covers the economic spectrum, so that the overall group responds to the fortunes of the economy. This is discussed further on pages 170–173. And, as shown on pages 177–180, the same can be true for bonds.

rose during that period by 153% (from $65 to $165). If you had simply put $50 into stocks and $50 into gold in 1973, your $100 investment would have grown to $166 at the end of 1977. Even though stocks did badly, the gain in gold had a bigger impact.

During 1981–86, gold fell 34% (from $590 to $390), while stocks rose 80% (from 78 to 140 in the NYSE Index). A $100 investment split evenly between stocks and gold at the beginning of 1981 would have grown to $146 by the end of 1986. Stocks gained more than gold lost.

More important, during the broader period of 1973–86, a $100 stock-and-gold portfolio would have grown to $435—even though stocks and gold each had bear markets within those 13 years.

Stocks and gold didn't cancel each other out. They complemented each other.

Broader Coverage Needed

Although a stock-and-gold portfolio would have done remarkably well, these two investments can't by themselves protect you from the economic time bomb. And the two-investment portfolio's good result at the end of the period hides the roller-coaster ups and downs you would have experienced along the way.

For more thorough long-term protection and for greater short-term stability, the portfolio needs to include long-term bonds and cash. Bonds will bring profits to the portfolio if there's a deflation. And cash helps to stabilize the portfolio during periods of tight money.

But the simple two-investment example illustrates a valuable principle: over broad periods of time, winning investments tend to have a greater impact on a portfolio than losing investments do—allowing the winners to pull the overall portfolio upward.[3]

[3]This may be more obvious if you realize that if one of the two investments rose by more than 100%, the portfolio would be ahead even if the other investment became worthless.

DISTRIBUTION OF PORTFOLIO

The Permanent Portfolio's success will be affected by the percentage of your capital you assign to each of the four investments.

No magic formula can tell you which distribution of investments will produce the best return over the next decade. And I think any attempt to be clever in assigning shares to the investments will do more harm than good.

I prefer the simplicity and impartiality of allocating 25% to each of the four investments. If you have, for example, $50,000 to put into the Permanent Portfolio, I would distribute it as follows:

Stocks	$12,500	(25%)
Gold	12,500	(25%)
Bonds	12,500	(25%)
Cash	12,500	(25%)

Each investment must have a substantial share, because the time will come when it must carry the entire portfolio. And each investment also will have bad periods, so no investment should have too large a share.

The portfolio's safety is underwritten by the contrasting qualities of the four investments—which assure that any event that damages one investment should be good for one or more of the others. And no investment, even at its worst, can devastate the portfolio, because it can't lose more than the 25% you've invested in it.

The Portfolio vs. Individual Investments

The graph on page 158 should help you visualize how the investments take turns contributing to the portfolio's profit and stability.

It shows how the Permanent Portfolio would have responded to the many changes in the economy between January 1970 and

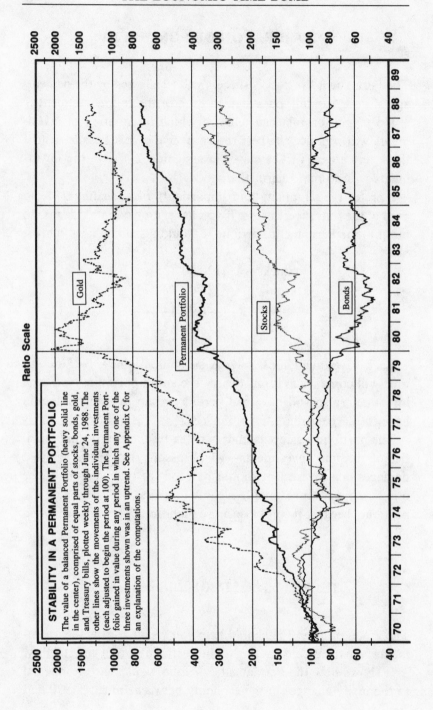

Ratio Scale

STABILITY IN A PERMANENT PORTFOLIO

The value of a balanced Permanent Portfolio (heavy solid line in the center), comprised of equal parts of stocks, bonds, gold, and Treasury bills, plotted weekly through June 24, 1988. The other lines show the movements of the individual investments (each adjusted to begin the period at 100). The Permanent Portfolio gained in value during any period in which any one of the three investments shown was in an uptrend. See Appendix C for an explanation of the computations.

Gold

Permanent Portfolio

Stocks

Bonds

June 1988. The graph also shows how the portfolio's three fluctuating investments—stocks, gold, and bonds—did during that time.

The portfolio's overall value rose whenever at least one of the three investments was in a major uptrend—even if the other two were falling. Whenever all three investments were falling, the portfolio drifted downward—briefly in 1973, 1974, and 1980; for 22½ months between 1980 and 1982; and for 12 months during 1983–84.

Over 18½ years of good times and bad times, the four-investment Permanent Portfolio did more than hold its own; it grew by 628%. That's a compound return of 11.3% per year. That's less than investment gurus promise, but it's a lot more than they can deliver consistently.

This average result doesn't mean the portfolio will gain 11.3% every year. In the best year, 1979, it gained 38.2%. In the worst year, 1981, it lost 6.4%. And the 11.3% figure is the average for the *past* 18½ years. The future will be different.[4]

Stability

Nonetheless, while the average return doesn't tell you next year's result, a striking feature of the graph is the Permanent Portfolio's stability. It achieved slow, steady, inexorable growth—sheltering its owner from the extremes that the individual investments went through.

The table on page 160 shows the portfolio's results for 1-year and 5-year periods from 1970 to 1987. Although the portfolio suffered one losing year during the two decades, there are no losing 5-year periods (or even 2-year periods).

The longest period during which the portfolio failed to move to

[4]During the 18½-year period, the average inflation rate was 6.4% per year—so the portfolio's average yearly return was 4.9% greater than the inflation rate. The method by which the portfolio's results were calculated is described on page 293.

FOUR-INVESTMENT PERMANENT PORTFOLIO
Long-Term Results

| Year | Result for Year | 5-Year Annual Average | |
		Portfolio	Inflation
1970	+ 4.6%	—	—
1971	+12.6%	—	—
1972	+18.9%	—	—
1973	+13.0%	—	—
1974	+13.1%	+12.3%	+ 6.6%
1975	+ 5.7%	+12.6%	+ 6.9%
1976	+11.0%	+12.2%	+ 6.9%
1977	+ 5.3%	+ 9.6%	+ 7.9%
1978	+11.3%	+ 9.2%	+ 7.9%
1979	+38.2%	+13.7%	+ 8.1%
1980	+13.6%	+15.3%	+ 9.2%
1981	− 6.4%	+11.5%	+10.1%
1982	+22.4%	+14.9%	+ 9.5%
1983	+ 2.8%	+13.1%	+ 8.4%
1984	+ 2.7%	+ 6.6%	+ 6.5%
1985	+19.5%	+ 7.7%	+ 4.8%
1986	+21.2%	+13.4%	+ 3.3%
1987	+ 5.2%	+ 9.7%	+ 3.4%

The annual results for the four-investment Permanent Portfolio described in the text. Each 5-year result is the yearly average for the 5-year period ending with the year shown. The results are hypothetical; the computations are explained in Appendix C.

a new high was 22½ months (between 1980 and 1982). And the deepest drop between any point and a later one was 15% (during 1980).

The absence of large or prolonged losses is especially remarkable for an 18½-year period that was so eventful. There were episodes of prosperity, recession, and rising and falling inflation—along with exciting booms, fearful crashes, and some boring drifts in the markets for gold, stocks, bonds, real estate, commodities, and foreign currencies.

Throughout all this, a Permanent Portfolio required no forecasts, rethinking, or timing—and it was far more stable than any individual investment.

Meaning of the Graph

The graph on page 158 isn't a prediction of future results. It's merely an opportunity to find out whether an idea that seems to make sense has already been disproven by experience.

The graph shows that the four-investment portfolio would have held its own during 18½ surprise-riddled years. The only economic climate that didn't show up during the 1970–88 period was a deflationary depression.

Every period in which the portfolio's value drifts downward is one of tight money—when *all* investments do badly. Even then, however, the interest-bearing cash in the portfolio softens the decline—saving the portfolio from the extreme losses suffered by the individual investments.

Too Much or Too Little

Keeping the portfolio divided about evenly among the four investments is essential to its success.

Except for cash, each of the investments—by itself—is extremely unstable. But the four together provide safety, stability, and steady growth.

Investing more than 25% in one investment would expose the portfolio to large losses—too large for the other investments to make up. You can see this in the movements of the individual investments in the graph on page 158.

Having too much in stocks would have dragged the portfolio downward during 1973 and 1974, when stock prices were cut in half—or during 1987, when the stock market fell 36% in just two months. Too much in gold would have devastated the portfolio between 1980 and 1982, when gold fell 60%. And bond prices lost 57% between 1972 and 1981. *Any* investment that dominates the portfolio will produce painful losses sooner or later.

It would be just as dangerous to have much *less* than 25% in any of the four. Doing so would weaken your wall of protection. Without stocks, you won't profit much from prosperity. Without gold, you can be ravaged by inflation. Without bonds, you lose protection against a depression. And without cash, you'll suffer severe losses during periods of tight money.

Keeping Your Hands Off

I realize that sometimes the prospects for one of the investments will seem particularly attractive. And you might be tempted to increase its share of the Permanent Portfolio to more than 25%.

But that's why you have a Variable Portfolio. Buy all you want of any investment for the Variable Portfolio, but don't change the Permanent Portfolio.

If it turns out that you were right about an investment's prospects, your Variable Portfolio will profit. But if events *don't* go as you'd expected, you won't lose one penny that's precious to you.

At times you may feel sure that one of the Permanent Portfolio's investments is headed downward. And you might be tempted to cut its share, or even get rid of it entirely.

Don't do it. If you expect the investment to fall, the Variable Portfolio can buy put options on the investment or sell it short. Any broker can show you how.

When you begin tinkering with the Permanent Portfolio, you throw away the security it is meant to give you.

YEARLY ADJUSTMENT

If you check the value of your portfolio at the end of a year, you'll find that changes in investment prices have caused two things to happen: (1) the overall value of the portfolio has changed; and (2) the portfolio no longer is evenly divided among the four categories. Some of the investments will be worth more than 25% of the portfolio's new value, and some will be worth less than 25%.

If it was proper to have 25% in each category at the beginning of the year, it's just as proper at the end of the year. So, once each year, you need to restore the portfolio to its original balance by returning each investment to a 25% share.

For each investment whose value now exceeds 25% of the portfolio's value, sell enough to reduce its share to 25%. Use the proceeds from those sales to buy enough of the other investments to bring each of them up to 25%.

It's easy to calculate how much you need to buy and sell. A simple worksheet (which you may not even need) is shown on page 164.

Importance of Adjustment

Making the annual adjustment keeps a Permanent Portfolio safe. When an investment has a good year, you have to divert some of its profit to the laggards—because you don't know what next year's laggards are going to be.

EXAMPLE OF A
PERMANENT PORTFOLIO ADJUSTMENT

(#1) Investment	(#2) Value Now	(#3) % Now	(#4) Designated %	(#5) Designated Value	(#6) Buy or (Sell)
Stock-market items	$ 17,320	27.7%	25%	$ 15,638	$ (1,682)
Treasury bonds	16,895	27.0%	25%	15,638	(1,257)
Gold	13,840	22.1%	25%	15,638	1,798
T-bills, money fund	14,497	23.2%	25%	15,638	1,141
Totals	$ 62,552	100.0%	100%	$ 62,552	$ 0

Column #1: Name of the investment.

Column #2: Current dollar value of the investment.

Column #3: Percentage of the total value of the portfolio represented by this investment.

Column #4: Designated percentage for this investment.

Column #5: Dollar value corresponding to the designated percentage.

Column #6: Dollar amount that must be bought or (sold) to bring the investment to its designated percentage.

If you neglect the adjustment, you'll own too much of the successful investment; the portfolio will be just as unbalanced as if you'd started with 35%, 50%, or more in a single investment. When the successful investment falls—as eventually it must—you'll take a beating.

And without the adjustment, some investment will have less than a 25% share—which will be too little for the investment to carry the portfolio when its time comes.

The graph on page 166 compares the progress of a portfolio receiving yearly adjustments with one that's never adjusted. The remarkable stability of the adjusted portfolio is missing in the unadjusted portfolio.

The unadjusted portfolio reaped greater profits in the 1977–79 bull market in gold. But that simply set it up for a tremendous fall during 1980–82, when the portfolio lost 43% of its value.

And with too much in gold, the unadjusted portfolio fell well behind the adjusted portfolio during the 1980s' bull markets in stocks and bonds. Because it continued to be so dominated by gold, the unadjusted portfolio didn't come back to life until gold perked up in 1985.

When to Adjust

The best time to calculate the adjustment is in December. After determining what needs to be sold, you can decide whether to make the sales immediately or wait until January—whichever gives you better tax results.

At other times of the year, if you're aware that one of the four investments has doubled in price—or declined by 50%—since the last adjustment, you may want to make an extra adjustment to restore the portfolio's balance immediately. It would be worth doing, but it isn't essential.

One adjustment per year is sufficient to keep the portfolio safe and profitable. So you don't have to pay any more attention to investment prices than you want to.

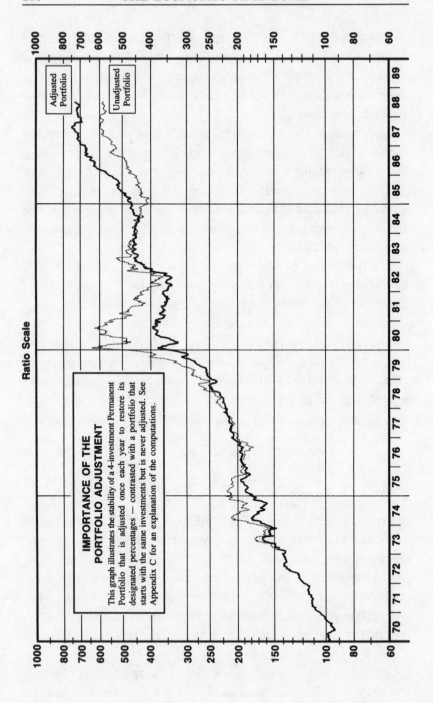

Ratio Scale

Adjusted Portfolio

Unadjusted Portfolio

IMPORTANCE OF THE PORTFOLIO ADJUSTMENT

This graph illustrates the stability of a 4-investment Permanent Portfolio that is adjusted once each year to restore its designated percentages — contrasted with a portfolio that starts with the same investments but is never adjusted. See Appendix C for an explanation of the computations.

WHO YOU ARE

Investment recommendations often are tied to such things as whether you're young, old, single, married, divorced, widowed, male, female, rich, poor, or have six toes on your left foot.

However, personal factors affect only one decision: how much of your capital is precious to you. So your age, family size, economic circumstances, and other census data should influence the way you divide your capital between the Permanent Portfolio and the Variable Portfolio. The freer you are to take risks, the more money you might choose to have in a Variable Portfolio.

But no matter what your circumstances, you need to protect whatever capital you decide is precious to you—the capital you can't afford to lose. Whether the Permanent Portfolio receives 50%, 70%, or 100% of your capital, its mission is exactly the same—to protect your precious capital in every climate.

So a 70-year-old retiree and a 27-year-old swinger need exactly the same kind of Permanent Portfolio. The differences in their needs and tastes will be reflected only in the share of capital each chooses to divert to a Variable Portfolio.[5]

SAFETY & PROFIT

So far, your questions may be outrunning my answers. We still need to explore:

1. How to buy and hold the four recommended investments—especially any that you've never owned before;
2. What to do about other investments you own now;
3. How to draw income from the Permanent Portfolio without compromising its safety;

[5]If you're retired, you may want to draw living expenses from the Permanent Portfolio. The way to do so is discussed on page 197. But as we'll see, there's no need to alter the portfolio's makeup in order to live off it.

4. How to minimize the portfolio's taxes;
5. How to keep the investments in the safest way;
6. How to do all these things without turning your life upside down;

. . . and more. I trust that all your questions will be answered before you finish this book.

Fortunately, putting together a simple, four-investment Permanent Portfolio isn't difficult. And for the small investment of time and effort, the reward is great. A balanced Permanent Portfolio is your best protection against the economic time bomb, because it will protect your capital no matter what the future brings.

The Permanent Portfolio isn't magic—a wonderfully simple way to get rich in a hurry. Nor is it a system for outperforming the investment markets. But it does allow you to be safe in economic climates that would be catastrophic for most investment programs—while continuing to profit in almost any circumstance.

With this kind of protection, you're free to walk away from your portfolio—to devote your attention to the things in life that interest you more. When you hear something scary on the evening news, you won't have to wonder whether you should make major changes in your investments. You'll know that, whatever the problem, your portfolio already deals with it.

14

Buying the Right Investments

The Permanent Portfolio I've described contains four types of investments—stocks, gold, bonds, and cash—with each receiving 25% of your capital.

Each of the four investment categories will be called upon, at some time, to carry the entire portfolio—stocks during a prosperous bull market, gold during inflation, bonds during a deflation, and cash during periods of tight money.

For your Permanent Portfolio to succeed, each investment must meet three qualifications:

1. The investment must be tied reliably to the economic climate it's meant to cover. For example, to respond to inflation you need gold itself—not a substitute, such as gold-mining stocks.
2. The investment must survive whatever comes. If you're depending on bonds to carry you through a depression, you can't hold bonds that might default when the going gets rough.
3. The investment must be highly volatile. Because you have

only 25% of the portfolio in the investment, it has to be powerful enough to lift the entire portfolio upward. You want stocks, for example, that will do *very* well during a bull market in stocks. Cash, because of its inherent stability, is the one exception to the need for volatility.[1]

Of course, volatility works both ways. An investment that can do especially well at times will do especially poorly when it's out of favor. But that isn't a problem for the Permanent Portfolio. If an investment takes up only 25%, the very worst it can do to the portfolio is to create a 25% loss—which most likely will be offset, at least in part, by a gain in another investment.

This chapter will show how the three requirements can be met, and provide the information you need to acquire the investments.

STOCKS

In choosing stock market investments, you must make certain that the 25% share you put into stocks will never fail to profit from a bull market.

To avoid such a disappointment, the stock-market budget must remain fully invested at all times, and the stocks you buy must represent the entire economy—not just one segment. Limiting yourself to industries you think will do best in the next bull market would risk the safety and effectiveness of your Permanent Portfolio—because you might guess wrong. The Variable Portfolio is the place to bet on the future.

In addition, you need stocks that are especially volatile, so that your holdings will be powerful enough to carry the entire Permanent Portfolio upward in the next bull market.

[1]A volatile investment is one that undergoes wide swings in price. When similar investments are rising, it goes way up; when similar investments are falling, it tends to fall further.

Mutual Funds

For most people, the practical way to acquire a broadly diversified group of volatile stocks is to split the stock-market budget among three to five properly selected mutual funds.

With mutual funds, a small investment can buy a position in scores of stocks that cover the entire economy. And a mutual fund makes it easy to invest exactly the amount called for by your stock budget, with no concern for round lots.

To be suitable for the Permanent Portfolio, a mutual fund should possess certain qualifications:

1. The fund should be diversified across the economy. It should *not* specialize in just one industry.
2. The fund should be virtually 100% invested in stocks at all times. You don't want to miss a bull market because a mutual-fund manager failed to recognize it. You want a fund that, *as a stated policy,* is always fully invested.
3. The fund should be highly volatile. You want it to be able to double in value—or more—during the course of a bull market, so that your stock investment will pull up the entire portfolio. To achieve that volatility, a mutual fund probably will emphasize smaller companies and growth stocks.
4. The fund shouldn't have a significant sales charge. Some funds charge a sales commission (called a "load") when you buy—anywhere from 1% up to the more common 8½%. Other mutual funds ("no-load" funds) charge no commission at all. You may find a fund whose unusual features or conveniences are worth a 1% or 2% commission. But avoid any fund that charges more. You don't need to pay a sales charge, since there are no-load funds that meet all the standards outlined here.

Seven no-load mutual funds that meet these qualifications are listed on page 232. Most require an investment of $1,000 or less to open an account. I suggest that you split the stock budget among three to five of them.

Put the same dollar amount in each of the funds you choose. Even if one seems more attractive or has a better performance record, you don't really know which fund will do best next year.

If a fund you've picked changes its investment policy someday, so that it no longer meets the qualifications I just listed, you'll have to replace it. Otherwise you shouldn't have to keep shopping for mutual funds after you've set up your Permanent Portfolio. Don't change mutual funds because one has been doing better than the others lately. This year's star may be next year's black hole.

Adjustments with Mutual Funds

Use the yearly portfolio adjustment (explained in the section beginning on page 163) to even out your holdings in the mutual funds. Although your Permanent Portfolio will start with equal amounts in each fund, some funds will be worth more than the others by the end of the year.

If the portfolio adjustment tells you to buy stocks, buy more of the funds in which your holdings have become the smallest—so that the stock-market budget becomes more evenly spread among your mutual funds. If the portfolio adjustment tells you to sell stocks, sell from the funds in which your holdings are greatest.

The adjustment doesn't have to equalize your mutual-fund holdings exactly. But you should eliminate any large differences. If one fund has done considerably better than the others during the year, you want to lock in some of its better performance. An outstanding result in one year is seldom repeated in the next.

Buying Stocks Directly

If you prefer to pick your own stocks, rather than buying through mutual funds, do so.

Spread your stock-market budget over at least a dozen sectors of the economy. Try to limit your selections to stocks that are especially volatile. A stockbroker can help by supplying a list of stocks with high "betas"—which is a measure of volatility.

You might want to consider putting a small portion of your stock budget into stock warrants. Warrants are, in effect, options to buy stock—but they have lives of many years, instead of only a few months. Their built-in leverage can add power to your stock-market budget. Your stockbroker may be able to tell you more about them and provide a list of available issues.

Remember that you're buying a selection of stocks to hold for many years. If you confine your choices to stocks that have rosy stories today, you may be shocked to see how out of date your selections have become tomorrow. Instead, look for volatile stocks within a wide range of industries.

Invest roughly equal dollar amounts in all of the stocks, but avoid odd lots if you can. As with mutual funds, use the annual adjustment to reduce your holdings of the one or more stocks that have done especially well.

If you find that holding stocks directly requires too much attention and effort, switch to mutual funds.

Stock Investments to Avoid

An investment in options on stocks or stock indices would require continual attention, and thus isn't suited to a Permanent Portfolio. In addition, option prices can go to zero—which would destroy your stock budget.

Futures contracts on stock indices also are ill-suited to the Permanent Portfolio. The contracts have to be rolled over periodically, and they don't have the kind of volatility that you can get—on a cash basis, without debt—from an aggressive mutual fund. No stock investment should be bought on margin, because the losses you'd suffer from the investment could far outweigh the gains in other investment categories.

GOLD

Although gold's primary purpose is to provide protection during a period of inflation, it also is the security of last resort—the one asset that isn't owed to you, but represents value in your hand. Gold is real money—portable, independent, divisible, durable, and recognizable. It survives when everything else fails.

Don't confuse real gold with any investment that's only indirectly related to gold—such as a share of a gold-mining stock. Gold stocks are *stocks*. Like other stocks, their values are affected by factors—such as company management, strikes, government policies, political unrest, and the like—that have nothing to do with U.S. inflation or the price of gold. Gold stocks can go down when gold itself is rising.

Nor should you invest the gold budget in numismatic coins, commemorative coins, or proof sets. Their price movements depend on the sentiments of collectors as much as on the price of gold. And commissions and markups are very high—in a completely different world from the costs of buying and selling stocks, gold, or bonds.

Gold Coins

Bullion coins are the most practical gold investment for the Permanent Portfolio. These are gold coins that are valued solely for the gold they contain. Unlike gold-mining stocks or numismatic coins, bullion coins move in lockstep with the price of gold bullion.

When you buy a bullion coin, you pay a small "premium" to cover the minting of the gold into a form that makes the weight and purity instantly recognizable. The premium normally is 3% to 5% or so of the price of the coin. When you sell the coin, you probably will get some or all of the premium back.

Several types of bullion coins are listed on page 176. All except the Krugerrand are widely available in the U.S.

The most prominent gold coins today are the American Eagles—which are minted by the U.S. Treasury. These coins are easily bought or sold. They come in four sizes—one ounce, ½ ounce, ¼ ounce, and ¹⁄₁₀ ounce—making it easy to use the precise number of dollars equivalent to 25% of your portfolio. Also, they are the only gold coin or bullion investment that can be kept in an Individual Retirement Account (IRA).

If your portfolio is large enough, there is nothing wrong with buying gold bullion as well as coins. But bullion must be bought in bars—the smallest of which is 32.15 ounces (one kilogram), equivalent to $12,860 at $400 per ounce.

Buying Gold Coins

Gold coins can be bought from coin shops—usually listed in the Yellow Pages under "Coin Dealers." On page 235, you'll find information on seven gold dealers that do business nationally. Each of them can ship the coins you buy to any location you specify. Safe storage facilities are discussed on pages 205–207.

Always get more than one quote before buying. Check the table on page 176 to see how large the premium on a coin should be. Don't stray very far from those premium percentages unless, for some reason, all dealers you contact are quoting a larger premium.

When you're given a price quote, be sure to ask whether it includes *all* commissions and other transaction costs. If there's any additional cost, add it to the quoted price before you decide which dealer to buy from.

Be wary of a price that's significantly *below* the prices of other dealers. Even if the dealer has a plausible explanation for his exceptionally low price, it's likely that you won't receive what you believe you're buying.

BULLION COINS
(Gold coins priced close to the value of the gold they contain)

Coin	Gold Ounces	Ask Price	Bid Price	Spread	Premium
American Eagle — 1 oz.	1.0000	$425.00	$414.50	2.5%	3.9%
American Eagle — 1/2 oz.	.5000	218.75	213.00	2.6%	6.9%
American Eagle — 1/4 oz.	.2500	113.50	110.50	2.6%	11.0%
American Eagle — 1/10 oz.	.1000	47.50	46.25	2.6%	16.1%
Canadian Maple Leaf	1.0000	425.00	414.50	2.5%	3.9%
S.A. Krugerrand — 1 oz.	1.0000	411.00	400.50	2.6%	0.5%
S.A. Krugerrand — 1/2 oz.	.5000	212.75	206.50	2.9%	4.0%
S.A. Krugerrand — 1/4 oz.	.2500	108.25	105.00	3.0%	5.8%
Mexican 50-peso	1.2057	505.50	489.50	3.2%	2.5%
Austrian 100 Crown	.9802	404.50	392.50	3.0%	0.9%

Gold bullion: $409.10 per ounce

Gold ounces: The weight of pure gold in the coin, not including any other metals the coin contains.

Ask price: The price at which you can buy from a dealer.

Bid price: The price at which a dealer will buy from you.

Spread: The difference between the bid and ask prices, stated as a percentage of the ask price.

Premium: The amount by which the ask price exceeds the value of the gold contained in the coin. Premiums fluctuate from day to day, but the premiums for these coins are likely to remain somewhat close to the levels shown. To calculate the premium, [a] divide the ask price of the coin by the ounces of gold in the coin; [b] divide the result by the price of gold bullion; [c] subtract 1; and [d] multiply by 100. For the American Eagle 1/2-ounce coin, for example, the calculation is: [a] 218.75 ÷ .5000 = 437.50; [b] 437.50 ÷ 409.10 = 1.069; [c] 1.069 − 1 = .069; [d] .069 × 100 = 6.9%.

Commissions may be charged in addition to the spread.

Source of prices: Monex International, Long Beach, California, October 14, 1988.

Gold Mutual Funds

There is only one mutual fund that invests in pure gold and would be appropriate for a portion of the Permanent Portfolio's gold budget. Information on the fund appears on page 237. Mutual funds that invest in the stocks of gold-mining companies are not appropriate for the Permanent Portfolio.

BONDS

Bonds are essential to a Permanent Portfolio. No other conventional investment can carry the portfolio during a deflationary depression.

During a deflation, investors will be eager to hold bonds, because the purchasing power of the dollar will be rising. But with so many borrowers in trouble, the demand for bonds will be directed toward the safest issues. Interest rates on the highest-quality bonds will plunge.

A newly issued $1,000 bond might pay interest of only 3%, or $30 per year—provided there's no credit risk. So investors would gladly pay as much as $3,000 to receive the $100 yearly interest paid by an existing 10%, $1,000 bond that had been issued by a borrower that still seemed reliable.

Even without a deflation, a mere decline in inflation causes bonds to appreciate, because interest rates usually decline in step with inflation.

Volatility

When interest rates fall, prices of existing bonds rise. How much a bond's price will rise depends primarily on how many years remain until the bond matures—when its principal is repaid. The more time remaining, the greater the bond's appreciation potential.

It's best to choose bonds with as long a time to maturity as possible. When interest rates are falling—especially in a depression—your portfolio will need as much profit as possible from the bonds. Very long-term bonds can be as volatile, and hence as profitable, as stocks.

Safety

The circumstances in which your portfolio will be relying the most on bonds—a deflationary depression—will be very difficult for many issuers of corporate and municipal bonds. Some corporations and state and local governments will be unable to repay their debts. This would place nearly all corporate and municipal bonds under a cloud of uncertainty and hold down their prices.

The bonds you own must be above suspicion. Not only will this assure that your bonds are safe, it also will assure that your bonds can appreciate dramatically at the time you're counting on them to carry the portfolio.

So it's essential that you hold only U.S. Treasury bonds. As explained on pages 41–42, no matter how bad its debt crisis becomes, the U.S. government remains the only institution that can print however many dollars it needs to pay its debts. So its bonds are the only dollar securities that have virtually no risk of default.

Interest from municipal bonds is exempt from federal income tax, but municipal bonds normally have smaller interest yields than taxable bonds do. Even if the after-tax return on a municipal bond is greater than that for a Treasury bond, stick with Treasuries. The slight difference in yield is the price you pay for safety and profit potential in bad times.

Buying Bonds

Treasury bonds are bought and sold in a large, liquid market, and are available from most stockbrokers. Prices vary from day to day, just as stock prices do.

The *face value* of a bond is the amount its issuer will pay at *maturity*—the day the principal is repaid. Bonds are available in various sizes, with $1,000 being the smallest face value. Prices are quoted as a percentage of the bond's face value. A price of 87, for example, means that a $1,000 bond is selling for $870.

The *coupon rate* of a bond is the interest the bond pays each year, stated as a percentage of the face value. Half that amount is paid every six months. For example, a $1,000 bond with a 9% coupon rate would pay interest of $90 per year—$45 every six months.

Prices of U.S. Treasury bonds are reported in the business sections of newspapers—usually in a listing headed "Treasury Securities." Look to the very end of the list to find the bonds with the longest time until maturity—usually 29 or 30 years.

The listing will show the coupon rate of each bond, the month and year in which the bond matures, and indications of recent buying and selling prices. The listing also will show the current *yield*—the interest the bond pays each year, stated as a percentage of the bond's current market price.

As you'll see from the newspaper listing, the yield will be roughly the same for all the bonds near the end of the list. Any issue that has a maturity at least 28 years away is suitable.

Every 5 to 10 years, you should sell the bonds you're holding and replace them with bonds that have at least 28 years or so until maturity. That way you'll always be holding bonds that can profit in a big way from a drop in interest rates.

Bond Mutual Funds

Some mutual funds invest in bonds, but no existing fund is appropriate for the Permanent Portfolio. You would need one that invested only in Treasury bonds, was 100% invested at all times, and held only bonds that had close to 30 years until maturity.

If you run across a new bond fund someday, don't buy it for the Permanent Portfolio unless it fits that description.[2]

CASH

U.S. Treasury bills are the best way to hold cash in a Permanent Portfolio.

Treasury bills (T-bills) are short-term debts, maturing in 52 weeks or less, owed by the U.S. government. Like Treasury bonds, they're virtually free of credit risk. To earn a higher yield than you can get from Treasury bills, you'd need to evaluate other investments for credit risk and watch them closely. And that's contrary to the spirit of a convenient, fail-safe, worry-free Permanent Portfolio.

The most convenient way to buy Treasury bills is through a stockbroker or commercial bank.

The minimum face value (the amount that will be paid to the owner on the day of maturity) of a Treasury bill is $10,000. Larger bills come in increments of $5,000—that is, $15,000, $20,000, and

[2]Benham Target Maturities Trust stays fully invested in zero-coupon Treasury bonds—a subject beyond the scope of this book. Since a zero-coupon bond is roughly three times as volatile as a normal bond, you could use the trust that has roughly 10 years until maturity. You can get information from Benham Target Maturities Trust, 755 Page Mill Road, Palo Alto, California 94304; (800) 472-3389 or (415) 858-3620.

so on. The price you pay for a Treasury bill will be less than its face value. The difference between the two amounts is the interest you earn. You don't receive interim interest payments.

Treasury notes or Treasury bonds that will mature within a year are perfectly acceptable in place of Treasury bills. Bonds and notes have the virtue of being available in minimum denominations of only $1,000, but the costs of buying and selling are a little larger.

Money Market Funds

Rather than buying Treasury bills outright, most investors find it more convenient to use a money market fund that invests in Treasury bills.

A money market fund is a mutual fund that invests in short-term debt securities—such things as Treasury bills, commercial paper, and bank CDs. The money fund earns interest on these securities, and passes the interest on to its customers in the form of a daily dividend.

Because safety—not interest yield—is our object, it's important that you use a money fund that invests *only* in Treasury bills or other short-term U.S. Treasury securities. For the Permanent Portfolio, you don't want a fund that is vulnerable to bank failures, corporate defaults, or anything else the economic time bomb might bring.

Most money market funds require only a small initial investment—usually $1,000. Additions or withdrawals can be made in almost any amount. This flexibility makes it easy to start your Permanent Portfolio with exactly 25% in a Treasury bill investment, and to return to that percentage precisely when you make the yearly adjustment.

Most money market funds allow you to redeem (sell) shares and withdraw money by writing a check, drawn on the fund, that you can deposit at any bank.

The flexibility of a money market fund makes it a convenient source of cash if you need to draw on your Permanent Portfolio for living expenses.

The $10,000 minimum for purchasing Treasury bills directly makes a money market fund essential for someone with a portfolio smaller than $40,000. Even investors with larger portfolios will find it easier to manage the cash budget if at least part of it is kept in a money market fund.

A list of money market funds that invest exclusively in Treasury securities appears on page 240.

HAVING THE RIGHT INVESTMENTS

I hope these details have illustrated the point that you can't build an effective Permanent Portfolio by simply throwing together a jumble of stocks, bonds, and other investments. Each investment, to contribute to a balanced and sturdy portfolio, must be volatile, able to survive, and tied directly to the economic climate it represents.

In addition, the investments must be stored carefully to ensure that they won't be lost in the turmoil of any crises we might face. We'll look at the task of safekeeping in Chapter 17.

15

Investments
You No Longer Need

The four-investment Permanent Portfolio I've described will keep you safe and sound in any economic climate. It makes certain that no disaster will be *your* disaster, and it offers the strong likelihood of steady, long-term growth.

You may be interested in other investments, however—perhaps because you believe that a particular item will do especially well in the coming months or years. If so, go ahead and buy it. That's what the Variable Portfolio is for.

Or you might be convinced that you should diversify the Permanent Portfolio further, in the hope of making it safer, by including additional investments—foreign currencies, real estate, foreign stocks, or something else.

Or you might own investments now that aren't easily disposed of—a business interest, annuities, partnership units, and so forth. Should these be integrated into the Permanent Portfolio, laid on top of it, or donated to the Salvation Army?

This chapter will discuss these possibilities.

The Virtue of Simplicity

One virtue of the four-investment Permanent Portfolio is its simplicity. This isn't a minor benefit. For most investors, it's essential.

A great deal of my attention over the years has been devoted to making the Permanent Portfolio as easy to implement as possible. Your investment plan won't succeed if you don't have the knowledge and talent to carry it out—or if your energy runs out before you finish setting it up—or if it's too much trouble to maintain after it's in place.

A reasonable case can be made for a more complicated, more sophisticated approach to a Permanent Portfolio. But any such plan, however attractive in the abstract, will be dangerous in practice if it requires expertise you don't have—or if it demands more effort and attention, year after year, than you'll be willing to give.

The simple, four-investment Permanent Portfolio will provide 90% of the safety and balance you might achieve by becoming a Permanent Portfolio monk and devoting your entire life to your investments. And it will give you far greater safety and balance than most investors enjoy.

Putting Investments in Perspective

As you read investment books, financial publications, and brokerage reports, you'll come across persuasive arguments for including this and that in your portfolio. Try to keep such arguments in perspective.

A logical, well-researched presentation might maintain that some particular stock will be "the investment of the 1990s"—like Xerox in the 1960s. And the argument may even be correct, but that's a matter for the Variable Portfolio.

Or you may read that some dire event is about to occur, and that your only hope is to have all your money in one particular investment. No matter how convincing the argument, I hope you'll notice that the four-investment Permanent Portfolio already covers you against *any* catastrophe. So you don't need to buy stock in Arks R Us. The Permanent Portfolio also will take care of you if, by chance, the event in question fails to occur—or shows up a decade or two late.

Or you may be told that a particular investment would enhance the safety of your portfolio. The plea may be a sensible one, in principle. But try to foresee how much the investment would complicate the job of managing your portfolio. If you attempt too much, you may wind up accomplishing too little.

And someone is sure to suggest that you might as well burn money in the fireplace as to buy Treasury bills and bonds when there are safe, triple-A investments that pay interest rates 2% or 3% higher. But I hope you'll remember that triple-A investments are safe in *normal* circumstances—and you don't want to have to monitor the economy's temperature, pulse, and blood pressure every week.

Finally, you're bound to receive sophisticated tax advice from all directions. Someone is sure to let you know that there are fancy annuities, tax shelters, and other devices that let you eat your cake and have it too—earn hefty returns and pay no taxes.

But calculate exactly how many dollars the plan would save in taxes. Then ask yourself whether that's a worthwhile return for compromising the safety of your capital by making yourself dependent on intermediaries, companies, and plans that may or may not survive the economic time bomb.

Coverage Against Events

It isn't by chance that the Permanent Portfolio contains four investments—no more, no less.

As discussed on pages 149–150, there are four basic circumstances for which you need to be prepared: prosperity, inflation, tight money, and deflation. While all investments are affected in some way by these economic climates, only the four I've suggested are so clearly tied to them in ways that you can rely on.

Before you add another investment to the portfolio, identify the investment's purpose. In which economic climate will it enhance protection and profit?

If there's no clear answer to the question, there's no reason to squeeze the investment into the Permanent Portfolio. And you may realize that you want the investment simply because you think it's going to be a winner—which would make it a candidate for the Variable Portfolio only.

If you do decide to add an investment to the Permanent Portfolio, then it must share a place with one of the four basic investments already there. The Permanent Portfolio should have 25% aimed in each of the four directions—toward prosperity, inflation, tight money, and deflation. Those climates are covered now by stocks, gold, cash, and bonds, respectively. If you add another investment, it must be funded from a specific 25%—not by drawing money away from all the categories.

For example, if you add an investment that you expect to do well during inflation, it must share the 25% allocated to gold. Don't split the portfolio five ways, giving 20% to each of five investments. That would make 40% devoted to inflation protection and only 20% for each of the other possibilities.

Most investments aren't clearly tied to a single economic climate in the way the four I've selected are. An investment that interests you might, for example, derive part of its potential from normal prosperity and part from inflation.

In that case, you'd need to make room for it by taking a little out of the stock budget and a little out of the gold budget. If you feel that allocating space for the investment this way is complicating things, you're right—but that's one of the prices you pay for straying from the basic program.

We'll take a brief look at a few of the investments that might be introduced to you as candidates for the Permanent Portfolio. Some of them make more sense than others, but I don't believe you need any of them. However, if one of them forces its attentions on you, I want you to know how to make room for it in the portfolio.

COLLECTIBLES

Collectibles are items that are prized for their rarity—such things as numismatic coins, rare stamps, fine art, and so on.

No strong link ties these investments to a single economic climate.

They do fairly well during a period of prosperity, because collectibles provide entertainment. During good times, people have more money to spend on the fun of collecting.

Collectibles usually have been at their best when prosperity and inflation coincide—when people are concerned about the future of the dollar but still have money to spend for enjoyment.

Although we haven't yet seen inflation above 25%, I doubt that it would be good for collectibles. Rampant inflation would impoverish millions of people. There could be distress selling of collectibles by many of them—who would be worrying more about finding dinner than about finding rarities. The mass market for collectibles probably would disappear.

If you include collectibles in your Permanent Portfolio, about two thirds of the collectibles' value should be counted in place of gold, and one third in place of stocks. But you'd be accepting a poor substitute for stocks—and a worse substitute for gold.

If you want to own collectibles, I hope you'll put them on your fingers, or on the wall, or in a display cabinet—anywhere but in your Permanent Portfolio.

SILVER

In the early 1970s, I bought silver because there was a worldwide shortage that the U.S. government had created by decades of interference with the silver market.

I bought silver at prices from $1.29 to $2.50 per ounce. In 1980, I sold at $38.

I may never again do that well with a speculative investment—although I'm still looking. In my affections, silver comes second only to my wife. It has played an enormous part in building my wealth and my reputation.

So I'm struck with a sense of déjà vu—not to mention nostalgia—when someone today says that a worldwide silver shortage will soon send silver to $100 or more. Loving silver as I do, I wish it were so. But the shortage ended in 1980, and there's no reason in the world for it to reemerge.

Silver no longer has the special investment status it had in the 1970s. It is now just another commodity—like wheat or copper. It will have bull markets from time to time. But the special circumstances that created the once-in-a-lifetime bull market of the 1970s aren't likely ever to be repeated.

Many investors believe silver is a twin of gold, but it's really only a third cousin. Silver is mostly an industrial metal, and only to a much lesser degree a monetary metal. Gold is mostly a monetary metal, and only slightly an industrial metal. The prices of the two have moved in opposite directions in the past 20 years more often than they've moved together.

If you believe silver belongs in your Permanent Portfolio, you'll need to carve a place for it by removing some of your stocks and some of your gold.

FOREIGN CURRENCIES

Major foreign currencies—the Swiss franc, the Japanese yen, the German mark, the Dutch guilder, and others—were big winners in the 1970s. And they had a second big bull market from 1985 through early 1988.

You may decide that foreign currencies would add something to your Permanent Portfolio. If so, they can be justified only as a hedge against inflation—an investment that will do well because the U.S. dollar is losing purchasing power. So any foreign currency investment for the Permanent Portfolio must be squeezed out of gold's 25%.

Your first choice probably should be the Swiss franc. Despite the greater attention given to the Japanese yen and the German mark, the franc has been the most volatile of the strong currencies, and thus the biggest winner when foreign currencies have reason to rise. It also is the foreign currency most likely to stand up to the world's problems.

In the bull market of the 1970s, the exchange rate of the franc rose 200% against the U.S. dollar, while the yen rose 100% and the mark rose 140%. In the bull market of 1985–88, the franc and yen each rose about 130%, while the mark rose 120%.

The safest and most efficient means for investing in the Swiss franc is by buying Swiss government bonds. In recent years, interest rates in Switzerland have been very stable, with the bonds usually yielding between 4% and 5%.

Swiss government bonds aren't sold in the United States. But you can buy them conveniently if you open a Swiss bank account (discussed on pages 206–207).

FOREIGN STOCKS

Foreign stocks became popular in the U.S. during the 1980s.

Market indices in some countries posted larger gains than the Dow Jones Industrial Average. But, in most cases, investor profits in foreign stock markets were no greater than in the U.S. stock market. Because the currency of the foreign market was appreciating against the U.S. dollar, the foreign market—when translated into U.S. dollars—showed a bigger gain.

The world's stock markets tend to go up and down together, so foreign stocks don't provide as much diversification as you might expect. And they might do worse than U.S. stocks during any period when foreign currency prices are declining—as was the case between 1980 and 1985.

If you do decide to hold some foreign stocks, you should fund them with money taken from the 25% devoted to U.S. stocks.

The easiest way to invest is through a mutual fund committed to investing only in foreign stocks. With a mutual fund, you're less likely to be ambushed while groping your way through exotic territory. And you'll get more diversification than you probably can achieve on your own.

However, you must be sure that what you buy really is a foreign stock fund—one that stays fully invested in foreign stocks at all times. If the mutual fund switches back and forth between U.S. stocks and foreign stocks, or switches between stocks and cash, it is a speculation on the fund manager's ability to foresee the future. That makes it a Variable Portfolio investment.[1]

REAL ESTATE

Your home is only incidentally an investment. It is primarily an item of consumption. You chose your present home because of where you wanted to live and how you like to live—not because you believed a specific house had a potential for price appreciation that no one else had recognized.

If you sell your home someday, most likely you'll reinvest any profit in a new home—again, one that will be chosen for reasons of consumption, not investment.

Because your home isn't primarily an investment, it shouldn't be treated as one. Its value is part of your wealth, but you would draw on that value only if a catastrophe forced you to sell. So you shouldn't count your home as an investment when planning either portfolio.

---

[1] I haven't found any foreign stock fund that stays 100% invested at all times as a stated policy. Three funds that come close to the standard are Transatlantic Growth Fund, Scudder International Fund, and T. Rowe Price International Fund.

If you believe that real estate is a good permanent investment, you might want to have something—apart from your home—in the Permanent Portfolio that would do well if real estate in general prospers.

But unless you're ready to go into the real estate *business,* it probably would be impractical (and possibly dangerous) to buy houses or apartments for that purpose. To avoid losing your shirt, you'd have to become an expert on real-estate investments in a way that isn't necessary when you buy stocks, bonds, gold, or Treasury bills. Buying investment properties for profit should be a profession—not a hobby.

A more realistic way to include real estate in your portfolio is to buy the stocks of real-estate investment trusts (REITs)—which are publicly owned companies that invest in real estate or mortgages. In general, when real estate is in a bull market, the REITs that invest in real estate itself also prosper.

Specify "equity REITs" (those that invest in property, not mortgages), and a stockbroker can supply you with a list of names.

Since real estate is likely to do best during periods of polite inflation—inflation rates of, say, 5% to 20%, in which the economy still operates somewhat normally—the money has to come from the gold budget.

SPECULATIVE INVESTMENTS

Of course, I can't cover here every investment that might come to your attention. It will be up to you to figure out the budget from which the money for any other investment must come. If you can't, perhaps you should pass up the investment for the Permanent Portfolio—while considering it for the Variable Portfolio.

One type of investment is wholly inappropriate for a Permanent Portfolio. That's an investment in someone's trading expertise.

An investment or managed account that hopes to profit by trading in and out of stocks or commodities or anything else is a bet on someone's talent. Even though *you* aren't attempting to outguess the future, you're betting that someone else can do so.

Such investments include commodity funds, mutual funds that switch between cash and stocks, and managed brokerage accounts. These are all speculations—the province of the Variable Portfolio. They don't belong in the Permanent Portfolio because the Permanent Portfolio doesn't speculate, and because these investments aren't tied irrevocably to specific economic climates.

Asset Allocation Funds

Some "asset allocation" mutual funds also are speculations on trading skill.

The Permanent Portfolio takes care of you by allocating assets one way once and for all. But mutual funds that switch capital from one investment category to another, as the managers believe the economic climate is changing, are merely a kind of speculative trading account.

They may be promoted as a way to achieve safety, but if you buy one, someone will be betting on the future with your precious capital. And it takes only one or two wrong guesses on his part to damage your wealth. Betting on a fund manager's expertise is prudent only if it's done with the Variable Portfolio.

ILLIQUID INVESTMENTS

Illiquid investments, including limited partnerships and your vested interest in a pension plan you don't control, are assets that can't be sold quickly and easily and at little cost.

I have two simple rules covering these investments:

1. If you don't have any now, don't buy any.
2. If you have some now, don't consider them to be part of the Permanent Portfolio.

Illiquid investments are in a different world from stocks, bonds, gold, and Treasury bills.

If you're receiving income from Social Security or an employer's pension plan, enjoy the income. But don't count the capital behind it as part of your wealth or part of the Permanent Portfolio—since you have no control over it.

A Business

If you own and operate a business, you should ignore it when planning your Permanent Portfolio.

It isn't a replacement for the stock market portion of the Permanent Portfolio—for the same reason that no single stock would be diversified enough. There's no guarantee that your business, or any one particular stock, will become more valuable during the time of a big bull market in stocks.

Enjoy the income that your business produces. But don't consider it to be part of your Permanent Portfolio.

ADDING TO THE PORTFOLIO

This chapter has discussed a number of investments you might find yourself considering for your Permanent Portfolio.

Although my tone has been negative, I don't mean to imply that all these investments are bad. My point is that they aren't needed for a well-balanced Permanent Portfolio.

You should ask yourself the purpose of an investment before buying it. Too often, one buys an investment because he's been told that it's a bargain, that it has a glorious future ahead of it, that it will pay a high yield, that it's safe, and/or that it will save taxes.

But name *any* investment and I'll make a persuasive case that it will accomplish such things. *Any* investment can be made to seem good.

Your only defense against the allures of Cambodian bonds or Telegenetic debentures or Australian greasy wool futures is to refrain from buying anything for the Permanent Portfolio until you've asked yourself these questions:

1. What does the investment offer? Safety? Profit?
2. In which economic climate will the investment enhance the portfolio? Prosperity, inflation, tight money, or deflation?
3. Is it an improvement over what you already have? Does it, for example, provide greater or more reliable protection against inflation than gold alone would provide?
4. If something promises a tax advantage, how badly do you need it? How much safety and convenience are you willing to give up for it?[2]

And if something seems like a bargain, it must be a speculation—as is anything that constitutes a bet on the future. I have nothing against speculations—provided they don't masquerade as investments.

For myself, I love to speculate, and that's why I have a Variable Portfolio.

[2]The tax ramifications of the four-investment Permanent Portfolio are discussed on the next page.

16

Living with
Your Portfolio

A Permanent Portfolio is easy to live with. It allows you to avoid heavy taxes conveniently, to make withdrawals from the portfolio for living expenses, and to absorb interest and dividends. And you can set up an easy-to-live-with Permanent Portfolio even if you have very little capital.

This chapter will cover these aspects of the portfolio.

SIMPLE TAX PLANNING

Safety is the first concern of the Permanent Portfolio. Profit comes second, and tax sheltering third.

You should turn your attention to tax planning only after you've assured yourself that the investments you've chosen are the safest possible. Fortunately, the four-investment Permanent Portfolio makes tax planning easy.

Gold produces no current income. And its price appreciation

195

won't be taxed until you sell. Even when you do sell (to make a portfolio adjustment), you'll be selling only part of your gold. And only a portion of what you sell will be a taxable profit; the rest will be a tax-free return of your investment.

The stock-market mutual funds I've suggested generally produce little in the way of dividends, because volatile stocks tend to forgo high yields in return for the possibility of rapid price appreciation. So the tax burden will be small—and, as with gold, will come mostly from sales made for portfolio adjustments.

Most of the Permanent Portfolio's potential tax burden comes from the Treasury bonds and bills. Bonds, bills, and most money market funds generate substantial interest income that is fully taxable every year. In addition, portfolio adjustments may create some capital gains for bonds.

Assuming an average interest rate of 10%, and assuming a maximum tax rate of 28%, your yearly tax bill normally should be no more than 2% of the value of your portfolio if you make no effort at all to reduce the tax burden. About 1½% of that is tax on the interest income, and another ½% allows for dividends and capital gains.

IRAs & Keogh Plans

If you can have an IRA (Individual Retirement Account), Keogh plan, or other pension plan that's under your control, you can reduce the tax burden considerably—perhaps to almost nothing.

Use the pension plan to hold as much of the bond budget as the plan has room for, so that each year's interest can be reinvested without being reduced by taxes. If there is any room left, put part of the cash budget into it. Leave some of the cash budget outside the plan—so that you can add or withdraw money freely, and so that you can make portfolio adjustments that involve stocks or gold.

For whatever portion of the cash budget you don't put into a pension plan, you may be able to reduce the tax burden by using the Treasury Bill Portfolio, which is a mutual fund (described on page 240) that minimizes immediate taxation.

No purpose is served by putting gold into a pension plan, since it doesn't produce yearly income that needs to be sheltered from taxes. And stock mutual funds should go into the pension plan only if you have room for them after housing most of the interest-bearing investments.

If you can shelter all the interest on the bonds and Treasury bills, the yearly tax should amount to ½% or less of the value of the portfolio.

Risky Tax Shelters

With a 28% maximum income tax rate, the built-in tax benefits of a Permanent Portfolio, and the effectiveness of the simple tax planning just explained, there's no need to reach for any fancy tax shelters.

Variable annuities, variable life insurance, or complicated, illiquid tax shelters will tie your future to investments that are less safe than Treasury bonds and Treasury bills. And they will weaken your Permanent Portfolio's power to protect you during a time of crisis.

INCOME FROM THE PERMANENT PORTFOLIO

If you choose, the Permanent Portfolio can supply cash for your living expenses.

Realize that it doesn't matter whether the cash you spend has come from interest, dividends, or capital gains (increases in the market value of your investments); it's still yours to use as you see fit.

The easiest way to withdraw money from the portfolio is to use a money market fund for at least part of your cash budget, and then write a redemption check periodically.

By the end of the year, your total cash holdings probably will amount to less than 25% of the value of the entire portfolio. When you make the portfolio adjustment and restore your cash holdings to 25%, be sure that enough of the 25% is in the money market fund to cover your withdrawal requirements for the coming year.

How Much to Withdraw

The amount you can safely withdraw from the portfolio each year depends on many factors.

The most likely performance for a Permanent Portfolio is an annual return (on average, over many years) that is about 5% greater than the inflation rate. For example, if inflation over the next 10 years should average, say, 7%, the portfolio probably would produce an average total return (from interest, dividends, and increases in the value of the investments) of around 12% per year.

There's no guarantee of this, of course. The actual results may be better or worse. But I believe that it's sensible to base your plans on a real, after-inflation return of 5% per year.

Thus, if you withdraw 5% of the Permanent Portfolio's current value each year, you can expect the portfolio's value—and the value of each withdrawal—to keep up with inflation. In other words, many years from now, after withdrawing 5% annually, your standard of living and the purchasing power of the portfolio should be roughly the same as they are today.

If you withdraw more than 5% per year, there may be periods when the portfolio's dollar value continues to grow but its purchasing power loses ground to inflation.

If you and your spouse have reached retirement age, and if you aren't concerned about preserving the full value of your portfolio for your heirs, you can prudently spend more than 5%. The portfolio will lose a little of its purchasing power every year—just as though you were drawing on an annuity that would take care of you so long as you live, but be worthless when you die.

Other Avenues

Whether or not you have a Permanent Portfolio, there are inescapable limits on how much income you can safely take from your investments without depleting your capital. A Permanent Portfolio doesn't make these limits any tighter, although it may make them more obvious.

For example, you might invest all your capital in bonds that pay 12% per year in interest, and spend all the interest each year. Your accountant will tell you that you're living off income and preserving the capital.

But inflation will be a fact of life, no matter how you invest. If inflation averages 7% per year (an example, not a prophecy), the high-yielding bonds and your annual income will have only 48% of today's purchasing power 10 years from now.

If you want more yearly income than a Permanent Portfolio seems to be able to give you, the problem is that your capital isn't sufficient to provide both safety and the income you want. Your only choices are to (1) live on less, (2) earn employment income in addition to your investment income, (3) draw down the capital over the years, or (4) take chances with an unsafe portfolio. These are the *only* choices.

An advantage of the Permanent Portfolio is that the money you withdraw from it won't be all taxable income. Part of what you draw will be a tax-free return of capital. So only part of what you spend will be taxable. As a result, you may need less gross income—because a smaller share of the income will go to the tax collector.

DIVIDENDS & INTEREST

The Permanent Portfolio will earn dividends and interest on stocks, mutual funds, Treasury bonds, and Treasury bills.

When you open an account with a stock-market mutual fund or a money market fund, you should choose the "automatic reinvestment" option so that the fund will use your dividends to purchase more shares for you. The dividends are part of the return on your investment, and they should stay with the investment until you make your next yearly portfolio adjustment.

When you receive dividends on stocks or interest payments from Treasury bills or bonds, you can endorse the check and deposit it into the money market fund that handles the cash budget.

If you are taking living expenses from your Permanent Portfolio, you should do it by withdrawing the money from the money market fund—which you can do just by writing a redemption check from the fund.

During the year, the value of your cash budget will drift away from its assigned share of the portfolio. The drift will come from the interest and dividends going into it, from withdrawals for living expenses, and from the performance of the other investments.

Don't let this worry you; at the end of the year, you'll make a portfolio adjustment and restore the cash budget to its assigned percentage.

HANDLING A SMALL PORTFOLIO

The Permanent Portfolio is almost as convenient for an investor with very limited capital as it is for a wealthy investor.

Suppose, to use an extreme example, that you have only $4,000 in savings with which to fund a Permanent Portfolio. Just as for any other investor, you should divide it four ways—$1,000 each in stocks, gold, bonds, and cash.

The stock-market portion can be invested in one mutual fund that has a minimum investment of $1,000, or it can be split between two or three funds that have smaller minimums.

The gold portion can be invested in American Eagle gold coins. If the current price of gold is, say, $500 per ounce, you probably could buy one 1-ounce coin (approximately $525), one half-ounce coin (roughly $270), one quarter-ounce coin ($140), and one tenth-ounce coin ($60).

The cash budget can go into a money market fund investing only in Treasury securities—one whose minimum is $1,000.

The only awkward category is the bond budget. You'll be able to afford a single $1,000 bond. But a bond's current price may be greater or smaller than its $1,000 face value, so you'll need to select a long-term bond whose actual price approximates your bond budget. Any discrepancy between your bond budget and the actual price of the bond should be added to, or subtracted from, the cash budget.

The yearly adjustments for the stock, gold, and cash budgets will be easy to make. The bonds will be a problem, because you can't split a $1,000 bond. The best solution is to make the adjustment so that bonds and cash together equal 50% of the portfolio. This isn't an ideal solution, but it's the only simple one available.

If your portfolio is this small, you most likely are adding to it periodically from your employment income. During the year, put the additions into the money market fund. When it's time for the yearly adjustment, you'll find that the extra cash means that you don't have to sell anything. Instead, you'll be able to rebalance the portfolio by buying stocks, gold, and/or bonds with the cash you added during the year.

If your portfolio is any larger—say, $10,000 or more—you should have no difficulty in setting up the portfolio or in making the yearly adjustment.[1]

[1]Another approach for small portfolios is to use a mutual fund that implements the Permanent Portfolio strategy. Information on such a fund is given on page 242.

17

Keeping the Investments Safe

How you buy and keep each investment can have a significant effect on the safety of the portfolio. You want to be sure each investment will actually be there when you need it.

Try to look ahead—not to predict what will happen, but to imagine what *could* happen. You must make sure that no disaster can take your investments away from you.

You can't wait until a crisis begins before you make the right arrangements. You'll have protection when you need it only if you've arranged it beforehand.

But, fortunately, safekeeping is a task that needs to be considered only once. And as soon as you've taken care of it, you're free to relax and forget about your investments.

Not only will you be safe in a crisis, but you'll have peace of mind when there isn't a crisis. When you hear that some dire event is about to happen, you won't have to worry whether it actually will. You'll know that you're safe in either case.

This chapter will look at each of the four basic investments I've suggested for the Permanent Portfolio—discussing how to hold them in the safest way.

STOCKS

Because stocks are in the Permanent Portfolio to profit from good times—not to protect you in a crisis—safekeeping isn't so critical as it is for gold or bonds, but it's important nonetheless. If your stockbroker goes broke during a crisis, taking your stock certificates with him, you'll lose part of your wealth.

The stocks a broker keeps for you are your property. Even if he goes bankrupt, your stocks shouldn't be affected—but you never know. If the broker has been borrowing assets from customers, in order to ward off bankruptcy, you could suffer a loss. And I don't think you should rely serenely on the Securities Investor Protection Corporation (SIPC)—any more than you should depend on the Federal Deposit Insurance Corporation.

The best and simplest protection is to ask your broker for stock certificates covering approximately two thirds of the shares of each stock. Keep these certificates in a safe-deposit box. The remaining shares—held by the broker in its name—will be available if a portfolio adjustment calls for a sale of stocks.

If your stock budget is in mutual funds, no special precautions are necessary or worth the trouble. Your ownership of shares will be recorded at each fund. There's no advantage to receiving share certificates.

GOLD

As discussed on page 174, the only gold investments appropriate for the Permanent Portfolio are gold coins and gold bullion. Each gives you ownership of the metal itself, rather than someone's promise or commitment to deliver it later.

The fact that your portfolio will be depending on gold in difficult times means that you should store the gold in a safe place.

Don't store gold for your Permanent Portfolio with a gold dealer in the U.S. Most gold dealers are honest and efficient, but several gold dealers have gone broke—taking their clients' gold with them. *There's no way you can judge the safety of a dealer's storage.* Even if the dealer claims that your gold will be insured or offers some other special guarantee, you won't know next month or next year whether that arrangement is still in place.

Any dealer worth buying from will ship your gold to any storage location you specify.

There are three storage possibilities I consider to be safe:

1. gold coins in your personal possession or in a safe deposit box;
2. gold bullion or coins stored with a U.S. bank acting as a custodian; or
3. gold bullion or coins stored in a Swiss bank.

Storage with a U.S. Bank

When a bank acts as a custodian, it will receive the gold shipped to it in your name by a gold dealer, and will hold the gold in safekeeping indefinitely. You will pay a small annual storage fee.

On page 236, you'll find a list of U.S. banks that store gold. Each of them deals directly with investors, and also with major gold dealers—who, as a matter of business practice, monitor the banks closely for safety.

The gold storage programs of these banks aren't interwoven with the banks' own finances. The gold is in a storage account, not a bank account. The gold isn't a debt the bank owes to you (as a bank deposit is); the gold is your property. So if the bank fails, your gold can't be claimed by the bank's creditors. At worst, a bank failure might create a few days' delay in getting your gold.

Gold in a Swiss Bank

Storing some of your gold in a Swiss bank adds geographic diversification to your Permanent Portfolio.

Owning gold outside the U.S. lessens your vulnerability to future actions of the U.S. government. If the government should ever decide to confiscate private gold holdings, as it did in 1933, all gold stored in public depositories in the U.S.—such as in banks—would be taken quickly.

Gold that's outside the country could be disposed of at your convenience. If you're required to sell, you might decide to wait a few months until you're satisfied that you can get the best price for your gold. I doubt that this would create any legal problems for you—although it would depend on how the confiscation law was worded.

A Swiss bank account offers privacy. It would have to be demonstrated that you're probably guilty of something that's a crime in both the U.S. and Switzerland before information about your account would be revealed by a Swiss bank.

But privacy isn't really the object. It can add immeasurably to your peace of mind just to know you own some assets that are beyond the reach of your government. In such a position, you don't have to worry quite so much when Congress seems to be hatching a new scheme for enriching the government at your expense.

The Swiss bank will buy and store the gold for you. If you specify that you want the gold kept in a custodial or safekeeping account, the gold will be your property, not gold that the bank owes to you.[1]

Discussing the ins and outs of a Swiss bank account would require a great deal more space than is available here. But on page 239, you'll find the names of three Swiss banks I've dealt with for

---

[1]Some Swiss banks also offer a "claim account." However, gold represented by such an account isn't your property; it's a debt the bank owes to you. Use only a custodial or safekeeping account.

many years. These banks are small enough to provide excellent service, have a great deal of experience in dealing with Americans, are liquid and safe, and can buy gold coins or bullion for you.

If you send an inquiry to any of these banks, you'll receive all the information you need to decide whether to open an account.

Diversifying Storage

Because gold is such a sensitive investment, I think it's important to diversify your holdings among storage locations.

A good arrangement would be to have a few coins hidden at home, some in a bank safe deposit box, and the rest in a Swiss bank account.

If you feel uneasy about any of these three arrangements, replace that one with storage at a U.S. bank. If, for any reason, you rely mainly on U.S. bank storage, split your holdings between two or more banks—if your holdings are large enough to allow it. Although the gold should be perfectly safe in all the banks, it's a good idea to hedge against the unthinkable and the unimaginable.

For many investors, buying and storing gold will be a new experience. If dealing with gold directly seems too exotic for you, an easier way to get started is by investing in a trust (which is similar to a mutual fund) that invests 100% in gold itself—not in mining stocks. Information on a pure-gold trust appears on pages 237–238.

BONDS

Treasury bonds are available in four forms, although not every bond issued is available in every form.

One of the four is as a credit in the Federal Reserve Book Entry System—a computer system operated by the Federal Reserve. If

you buy a bond directly from the Treasury (at an auction con-
ducted by the Federal Reserve), your name will be in the computer
as the owner.[2]

The second method is to purchase the bonds through a stockbroker (or bank), and leave them on deposit with the broker. In
that case, the broker's name will be in the Federal Reserve Book
Entry System. Your ownership will be recorded on the books of
the broker.

The third and fourth forms involve certificates of ownership.
Certificates are either "registered" or "bearer."

If the certificate is registered, your name is on file at the U.S.
Treasury as the owner. You can sell the bond only by endorsing
it over to your broker (or to the buyer).

A bearer bond is a certificate with no name on it. Like cash, it's
the property of the bearer—whoever holds it.

A certificate, whether registered or bearer, can be lost or stolen.
A registered certificate is much less attractive to a thief, since it's
harder to resell without proper identification. If a registered certificate is lost or stolen, you can get a replacement upon posting
a surety bond—the cost of which may be roughly 5% of the value
of the bond. But if a bearer bond is lost or stolen, it's gone; you
have no remedy.

You can obtain certificates for your bonds—either registered or
bearer—by buying the bonds from a stockbroker, and then re-
questing delivery of certificates.

You'll probably get some resistance when you do this. Brokers
don't enjoy handling certificates. In fact, most of them don't enjoy
dealing in Treasury securities at all, because the commissions are
so small (usually no more than 0.5% for bonds). They'd prefer to
sell you other kinds of bonds.

Even so, I believe the safest way to keep a Treasury bond is as
a registered certificate that's stored in a place you consider to be

[2]You can obtain literature explaining how to buy bonds directly from the Treasury by
writing or calling the U.S. Treasury Department, Bureau of the Public Debt, Department
A, Washington, D.C. 20239-1000; (202) 287-4113. Ask for an information packet covering
direct purchases of Treasury bonds.

safe—such as in a safe deposit box. The registration allows the certificate to be replaced (at a cost) if it's lost. And the certificate assures that even a computer foul-up won't cloud your ownership.

Next in order of safety is a bond purchased at a Federal Reserve auction and kept in the Federal Reserve Book Entry System. The only danger here is the possibility of a computer problem that muddies the record of your ownership.

Third choice is a bearer certificate stored in a place you consider to be safe. If no place seems secure enough, don't ask for a bearer certificate.

The weakest of the four forms of ownership is a bond registered in the name of a U.S. bank or broker. Although the bond, in principle, is your property, you're vulnerable to any financial problems of the broker that might lead to hanky-panky.

Even though keeping bonds with a broker is the *least* safe alternative, it isn't *un*safe. You'll find it convenient to keep a share of your bonds—not more than one third—stored with a broker, for easy handling when you make a portfolio adjustment.[3]

CASH

If you buy Treasury bills directly, rather than through a money market fund, you can buy them from the U.S. Treasury or through an intermediary—such as a stockbroker or commercial bank.

By buying from the Treasury, you eliminate reliance on an unnecessary intermediary. You can obtain the literature that explains how to do this by writing or calling the U.S. Treasury Department, Bureau of the Public Debt, Department A, Washington, D.C. 20239-1000; (202) 287-4113. Ask for the information packet covering direct purchases of Treasury bills.

[3]If you buy U.S. bonds through a Swiss bank, the bank normally will buy and keep them through a U.S. broker or U.S. bank. So this is slightly less safe than buying directly from a U.S. broker—since one more intermediary stands between you and your bonds.

Money Market Funds

A money market fund matches its maturities precisely. Every "deposit" with the fund is a demand deposit, because the customer can ask for his money at any time. And all of the fund's assets are marketable, short-term securities that can be turned into cash whenever necessary, without loss—so long as the securities themselves don't go into default. So a money market fund is completely liquid.

A fund that invests only in short-term U.S. Treasury securities has virtually no risk of loss. Thus, no matter what might come, your cash should be safe.

Bank Holidays & Runaway Inflation

If, in a banking crisis, the government ordered all banks to close, you wouldn't be able to obtain money from a money market fund (or from any other investment, unless you sold it to someone for cash). You probably wouldn't be able to cash a check, because banks wouldn't be paying out money. Your investment in a money market fund would be safe but temporarily out of reach.

I believe it's prudent to keep a small supply of cash somewhere safe for such an emergency. Ideally, you'd have enough cash to cover two weeks of normal expenses.[4]

Also, as a very small part of the cash budget, it might be prudent to hold some "junk silver coins"—U.S. dimes or quarters that were minted prior to 1965. These coins are 90% silver (unlike the copper-nickel coins in circulation today), and they sell at a price based on the current price of silver bullion. They have no numismatic value.

---

[4]During the bank closing of 1933, banks were physically open to the public, and safe deposit boxes were accessible—making them a safe place to keep cash. But there's no guarantee this would be the case the next time.

A small quantity of silver coins (400 or 800 quarters, for example) covers the remote—but not farfetched—possibility that a runaway inflation might destroy the usefulness of paper money. In such an event, pre-1965 U.S. silver coins could emerge as the only practical spending money.

Checking Account

Because of the shaky condition of the banking system, I don't want to have money I can't afford to lose in any bank.

Some investment advisors and companies will show you how to evaluate the safety of a bank, or will evaluate a bank for you. But bank financial statements don't include the information about loan maturities and loan collateral needed to gauge a bank's strength. So I wouldn't want to depend upon such an evaluation.

In any event, it isn't necessary to rely on a bank—even for the non-investment money you use for living expenses. You can use a money market fund without sacrificing the convenience of a checking account.

Most money market funds give you a checkbook, and allow you to withdraw money from the fund simply by writing a check—just as you would write a check drawn on your own bank account. All money market funds restrict check-writing in some way—either by limiting the number of checks you can write each month, by requiring a minimum check size (typically $500), or by charging a fee for each check.

You can keep a checking account at a local bank, but deposit most of your income into the money market fund. Pay your bills by writing checks on the bank account. As needed, write a single check on your money fund account, large enough to cover the bank checks you've written, and deposit the money fund check in your bank account.

A bank failure could hurt you only if it occurred between the time you deposited the money fund check and the time the bank checks cleared—in which case you could lose the sum represented by whatever checks hadn't yet cleared.

You can escape even that possibility by arranging an overdraft agreement, or "ready reserve account," with the bank. This would allow you to write bank checks whenever you need to, and deposit the money fund check after they've come back to your bank and created a negative balance in your checking account.

This eliminates your vulnerability to the bank.

SUBSTITUTES

As you shop for the investments you need, you may be offered substitutes.

A broker might tell you that you should use his money market fund instead of investing in Treasury bills or in a T-bill-only money market fund. He'll point out the convenience, and he'll certainly have a slightly higher yield to offer. But he won't be offering the same safety.

A rich uncle will explain that interest on municipal bonds is exempt from federal income tax, but he won't mention (if he even realizes it) that the bonds wouldn't be 100% secure in a crisis.

And someone will tell you that gold stocks are more volatile than gold bullion and bullion coins—and that "penny stocks" are the most volatile of all. But he may not tell you that gold stocks don't rise at all in the severe circumstances that call for gold's protection.

For over two decades, I've been thinking about these investments—about their potentials, their vulnerabilities, and their alternatives—and about the conditions that could descend upon the economy in a crisis. You might not draw the same conclusions from the information as I have. But if I've omitted some alternative in this book, it probably isn't because I've never heard of it or considered it.

SAFEKEEPING

As you set up the Permanent Portfolio, try to imagine everything that might go wrong. Ask yourself how you can eliminate your vulnerability to whatever ominous possibilities occur to you.

Wherever convenient, diversify by storing investments in two or more places.

If something you're about to do makes you uneasy, try to identify the source of your uneasiness. See if there's a way to neutralize the anxiety—perhaps by diversifying further.

18

How to Speculate Safely

The Permanent Portfolio is designed for protection, and is funded with the money that's precious to you. Once established, it remains unchanged—except for the annual portfolio adjustments that restore the original investment percentages.

For the Permanent Portfolio to do its job of providing safety, you must be a little dumb about running it. You must resist any temptation to be clever, or to tune the Permanent Portfolio to match your opinions about the future—opinions that are certain to change from time to time.

It is in the Variable Portfolio, if you decide to have one, that you try to outwit the investment markets. Almost the opposite of the Permanent Portfolio, the Variable Portfolio is funded only with money you can afford to lose—not money you would be glad to lose, but money you could endure losing.

For the Variable Portfolio, the Court of Review is always in session. Its holdings will change, perhaps frequently, as you make new decisions about which investments are best to own at the moment. You put an investment in the Variable Portfolio if you believe it will be especially profitable, and if you're willing to bear the risk of being wrong.

This chapter may help you decide whether to have a Variable Portfolio. A careful decision will make it easier for you to treat your Permanent Portfolio with the hands-off respect it deserves.

WHAT IT DOES

The Variable Portfolio lets you bet on the future in the hope of making a big profit or a quick one.

If you believe that the world is running out of silver, your Variable Portfolio could buy some. If you decide a particular company is going to run rings around its competitors, you could buy stock in it. Or if someone convinces you that the country is about to be overrun by mice, you could use your Variable Portfolio to buy a cat farm.

If you like to play the commodities market or deal in stock options with split-second timing, do it with the Variable Portfolio. If you believe that technical analysis, cycle theories, market indicators, or any other system can show you when individual stocks will rise or fall, try to profit with the Variable Portfolio.

Whenever you think you know which way a particular investment is going and want to try to make money on it, the Variable Portfolio is the vehicle for your wager.

How to Use It

Unlike the Permanent Portfolio, anything goes in the Variable Portfolio.

There are no restrictions, no vows of celibacy, no wet blankets like me trying to ruin your fun. You can use any strategy or system you want—from exhaustive fundamental analysis to Tarot cards.

You can make long-term bets or short-term speculations.

You can buy an investment that also happens to be in the

Permanent Portfolio. But when you sell it from the Variable Portfolio, don't touch your Permanent Portfolio holdings.

You can buy on margin if you want to. But make sure your
maximum potential loss is limited to the amount you have in the
Variable Portfolio.

You can add capital to your Variable Portfolio with income
from your salary or business. But never draw on the Permanent
Portfolio to cover the Variable Portfolio's losses.

At times, you might have just one investment in the Variable
Portfolio, or you might have many. And sometimes the entire
portfolio will be in cash—when no investment tickles your speculative fancy.

You don't have to worry about safety, because you aren't betting funds that are precious to you. You could even keep idle
Variable Portfolio money in a savings & loan.

This isn't an invitation to be reckless with the Variable Portfolio. It's only a reminder that you can never be hurt badly by
what happens to the Variable Portfolio—if you haven't allocated
too much of your capital to it and too little to the Permanent
Portfolio. You don't have to agonize over the Variable Portfolio's
safety, because you aren't placing your financial future in jeopardy
when you make a Variable Portfolio investment.

RECOGNIZING THE DIFFERENCE

Many investment plans that are promoted as conservative and safe
are really speculations.

They depend upon your foresight or your investing talent, or
the foresight or talent of an advisor, or the accuracy of a market
indicator. Anything that attempts to outguess the investment markets is a speculation, and so the Variable Portfolio is the place for
it.

If you think you can outperform the stock market by using
some market signal to switch back and forth between a mutual

fund and a money market fund, that's a Variable Portfolio speculation.

If you believe you can identify investment trends by studying
price graphs, you should do it with money from the Variable
Portfolio.

If you think a particular mutual fund will time its investments
well enough to outperform the stock market, invest in the fund
with the Variable Portfolio.

If there's a hotshot broker or investment advisor who's making
a fortune for everyone in the world but you, open a managed
account with him—but do it with money from the Variable Portfolio.

If you believe real estate is the world's best investment, and you
think you can get rich by buying and selling houses, use the
Variable Portfolio for the purpose.

I'm not recommending any of these things. I just want to make
sure that you never bet on them with precious capital—capital
that belongs in the Permanent Portfolio.

You bet on your expectations and your talent with the Variable
Portfolio; if you do well, you might earn above-average profits.
With the Permanent Portfolio, you leave your judgment, your
expectations, and your talent at the door.

STRATEGY

Even though the Variable Portfolio isn't governed by any inherent
restrictions, you obviously want to do as well with it as possible.
You'll put yourself ahead of the game if you establish clear standards for judging speculations—for deciding when a particular
opportunity has sufficient potential to warrant taking the plunge.

Otherwise you may find yourself buying anything that looks
good and keeping it forever. Since most opportunities don't live
up to their advance billing, your losses could easily outnumber
your gains—and your average loss may be greater than the average gain.

To make the most of your Variable Portfolio, you need a set of rules that cover such things as:

1. How good an opportunity must be to make it worth betting on.
2. How much of the Variable Portfolio to devote to an investment in a given situation.
3. How you'll know when to "bail out" of a losing investment—rather than letting the loss accumulate.
4. How you'll decide when to take profits on a winning investment.[1]

TO HAVE OR NOT TO HAVE

I believe that everyone needs a Permanent Portfolio. Even a free-swinging speculator should have a Permanent Portfolio as a safety net.

But not everyone needs a Variable Portfolio. I know many investors for whom a Variable Portfolio would be inappropriate. Should *you* have one?

If you're ever going to be tempted to base an investment decision on your judgment about the future, the answer is an emphatic *yes.* Without a Variable Portfolio, you'll find yourself tinkering with the Permanent Portfolio every time you think you see trends changing. That's dangerous, because there's no limit to it. The existence of a Variable Portfolio makes it easier for you to keep your hands off the Permanent Portfolio.

But if you have no interest in speculating on the future, if you're sure you won't delay buying something for the Permanent Portfolio until "the time is right," then you don't need a Variable Portfolio. If you want to be able to establish an investment pro-

---

[1]The strategy I use for my own Variable Portfolio, and for the speculations I suggest in my newsletter, is too extensive to go into here. But it is summarized in *Why the Best-Laid Investment Plans Usually Go Wrong,* described on page 245 of this book.

gram and then forget about investments entirely, don't complicate your life by setting up a Variable Portfolio.

HOW MUCH IN THE VARIABLE PORTFOLIO

If you decide to have a Variable Portfolio, you will need to decide how much money to put into it.

The maximum amount you can use is the amount you're willing to lose. You may not lose everything in the Variable Portfolio; in fact, you're hoping to make a big profit with it.

More often than not, such hopes are disappointed. The one cardinal principle I hope you take away from this book—more than any other—is that you should never bet on the future with money you can't afford to lose. Money that's precious to you must be invested in a fixed, balanced portfolio that will survive any economic climate.

If you decide on a figure that you're willing to risk, you don't need to use all of that for the Variable Portfolio. Whether you do might depend on how much confidence you have in your ability to make money with the Variable Portfolio, or how much time and effort you want to give to the task.

I hope you make a fortune with your Variable Portfolio. But, when deciding how much to put into the portfolio, realize that *you may actually lose all the money.* So don't take out a home equity loan to finance the Variable Portfolio.

THE CRISES

One avenue for the Variable Portfolio may be to bet on the economic time bomb—if you believe you can judge how and when the crises will unfold. There are a number of investments that might, *at the right time,* be very profitable for the Variable Portfolio.

If you think a banking crisis will erupt soon, you could buy put options on banking stocks.[2]

When the inflation-recession seesaw seems to be tilting toward inflation, buy gold or call options on gold.

When the seesaw seems to be tilting toward recession, buy put options on stocks or stock-market indices.

If you think the debt crisis is about to lurch out of control, buy put options on government bonds.

If a crisis seems to be brewing, but you believe it will prove to be a false alarm, consider buying junk bonds—which would profit greatly if interest rates fell sharply.

Or if you think the economic time bomb will turn out to be a dud, and that the economy will muddle through its problems, buy the stocks of companies that ought to profit the most.

And if you think insiders are looting the investment markets, become an insider.

[2]A put option is a security that profits if a particular stock goes down in price. Since options have very short lives (usually no more than 9 months), they frequently expire worthless. So any investment in options should be with only a small portion of the Variable Portfolio; otherwise you could lose the entire portfolio in a matter of months. A stockbroker can provide information about the way options work.

19

Getting Started

T o establish an investment program, you need to:

1. Determine how much of your capital is precious to you.
2. Divide your capital between the Permanent and Variable Portfolios.
3. Choose the investments for the Permanent Portfolio.
4. Compare the investments you've chosen with what you own now.
5. Sell what you have that you don't want.
6. Buy what you want that you don't have.

HOW MUCH YOU HAVE AVAILABLE

To begin, you need to make an accurate estimate of the investment capital you have to work with. So I suggest that you make a list of all your investments.

What to Include

The list should include:

1. stock market investments and mutual funds
2. bonds of all kinds
3. gold bullion and coins
4. bank accounts and certificates of deposit
5. money market fund accounts
6. real estate held for investment purposes
7. limited partnerships and/or tax shelters
8. the cash value of annuities and life insurance policies
9. collectibles (that aren't kept as a hobby)
10. foreign currencies
11. commodities
12. managed investment accounts

. . . and so on.

What to Leave Out

Do *not* include any of these items on your list:

1. your home
2. term life insurance policies
3. checking accounts you use for paying bills
4. debts owed to you by friends or family, unless you're sure they'll be repaid in the very near future
5. a business you own and operate, unless you're thinking seriously about selling it
6. the capital value of a pension plan, unless you control how the plan invests
7. the value of anything else that can't be converted to cash
8. anything you own for personal use only (such as your furniture, your car, jewelry, and so on)

Values

For each item you put on the list, note the quantity you own—200 shares of a stock, 386.124 shares of a mutual fund, 12 Krugerrands, and so forth. Look in the newspaper, or in a recent brokerage account statement, for the current unit price of each of your investments that's listed there. Determine the market value of each item by multiplying the quantity you own times the current price.

If you own annuities or other investments that aren't listed in the newspaper, estimate their minimum liquidation value—the amount you could count on getting if you closed out the investment now. Don't leave something out simply because you have no intention of selling it.

Deduct from the value of each investment any debt that may be associated with it. This includes mortgages, margin loans on stocks, loans made against annuities, and so on.

Then add up the net market value of all the investments and see what your capital amounts to. Deduct 3% from the total as an estimate of the costs that might be involved if you sell, and for price declines that might occur while you're planning your portfolio.

This final result is your available capital. This is the sum of money with which you can create a Permanent Portfolio and, possibly, a Variable Portfolio.

THE IDEAL PLAN

The next step is to decide on the investment plan you should have.

I believe the best approach is to put the money you can afford to lose into a Variable Portfolio, and keep the rest of your capital in a Permanent Portfolio—distributed equally among stocks, gold, bonds, and cash.

But I'm not going to live with the consequences of your decision; you are. So the decision has to be one with which you'll be comfortable.

The best way to decide what your investment program should look like is to imagine that you have a clean slate to work with. You should identify what is best before you decide what is possible. And you can't think objectively about what's best if you're influenced by the constraints of your present situation.

Start by imagining that you've sold every investment you own. Pretend that every item on the list you just made has been converted into cash. Now you don't own *any* investments—no stocks, no bonds, no real-estate speculations, no limited partnerships, no annuities, nothing. And all your debts are paid. Your investment capital is just one large pile of cash, waiting for you to tell it what to do.

In other words, if the figure at the bottom of your list was $67,428.32, think of it as $67,428.32 of cash to be invested—not as $67,428.32 worth of investments you already own.

In this all-cash position, you're free of all your past decisions—which shouldn't dictate the decisions you make now. You can invest your money according to what you know and believe today—without having to work around any investment, large or small, that you bought yesterday.

What will you do with that freedom? How will you invest the money? What do *you* think makes sense? How much should you have in stocks? How much in bonds? Gold? Cash? Other investments? What kind of program—which investments and how much of them—is needed to make you feel safe?

How much do you want to set aside to play with—to bet on investment trends? How much can you comfortably risk on such speculations? How much can you afford to lose without disrupting your life? In other words, how much should you set aside for a Variable Portfolio? Or is there any reason for you even to have a Variable Portfolio? (If you're going to have a Variable Portfolio, the investments that might go into it someday are of no concern right now. All you need to think about is the share of your investment capital you want to risk.)

Take your time with these decisions. As you think about the questions, make notes. Write down the percentages of capital you think you should have in each investment. Change them if they make you nervous. It may be a day or two, or more, before you finally arrive at a plan that doesn't create some uneasiness and invite further revision.

As you consider any particular arrangement, imagine that it already exists. Would you feel safer? Would that plan allow you to relax and enjoy your life—feeling that your capital is secure? Would you be able to walk away from it and forget about it—with no fear that unfolding events would force you to come back and make changes?

When you have the plan that produces "yes" answers to those questions, you've arrived at the Ideal Plan—the safest, most secure investment program you can imagine.

Split Between the Two Portfolios

One of the most important decisions you have to make is how you'll divide your investment capital between the Variable Portfolio and the Permanent Portfolio.

When you reach a tentative decision, there are two questions to ask yourself to find out whether the tentative decision is correct. You should ask both questions. If either answer is unsatisfactory, alter the decision and ask both questions again.

First, regarding the amount you're thinking of allocating to the Variable Portfolio, how will you feel if you lose every penny of it? Will your plans for the future be destroyed? Will you tell yourself that you're a fool? Will you tell your spouse at all?

Approaching the matter this way will encourage you to keep the Variable Portfolio small. It isn't a cheery exercise, but it may save you more serious grief later—since you really can lose all the money you put into the Variable Portfolio.

Then approach the matter a second way. With the division of

capital you're considering, will you be able to keep your hands off the Permanent Portfolio? Or will you want to change the Permanent Portfolio whenever you see an investment you think is going to be a big winner? Will you be able to stand aside stoically and do nothing when you think one of the Permanent Portfolio's investments is about to take a dive? Or, worse yet, when you see it already leaving the diving board?

Asking this second question will encourage you to have a larger Variable Portfolio—to provide an outlet for your forecasting urges while preserving the integrity of the Permanent Portfolio.

It may take a while to settle on the correct split between the two portfolios. For each division of capital you consider, ask both questions. You'll have the perfect split if you can contemplate losing everything in the Variable Portfolio without anxiety—and also feel confident that you won't be rearranging the Permanent Portfolio the next time you hear a persuasive story about what's hot and what's not.

THE REAL PLAN

Once you've arrived at the Ideal Plan, you can move on to a real plan. You may have to make difficult decisions to reconcile what you want to do with what you have to work with.

For one thing, you may have trouble putting the Ideal Plan in practice because of illiquid investments you own—real estate speculations, limited partnerships, and the like. If any of them didn't wind up in the Ideal Plan, will you keep them? Will you put any of them into the Variable Portfolio? Or will you sell them and make a fresh start?

Are there any other constraints that you'll continue to accept, that will require that you deviate from the Ideal Plan? If there are constraints you won't eliminate, you'll need to revise the Ideal Plan to allow for them.

But before you make any compromises with the Ideal Plan, you should clearly identify what each compromise is. How much are you giving up in safety, convenience, or simplicity? Precisely how many dollars will a higher interest yield or other benefit actually deliver to you each year in exchange for what you're giving up?

Then take a last look. It's important that *you* be satisfied with the plan. Not only must it take care of you in a crisis, it must be easy to live with every day before then. If what you own makes you edgy, you own the wrong investments. A safe portfolio isn't supposed to raise your blood pressure, it should lower it.

Once you've settled on your plan, you need to sell whatever you own now that isn't part of that plan. Use the proceeds of those sales to buy the elements of the Permanent Portfolio that you don't own now, or set some of the proceeds aside for the Variable Portfolio.

DOING SOMETHING TODAY

No one can know when the next crisis may erupt. So it's important that you have some assets now that will insulate you from whatever happens.

If implementing your Ideal Plan seems too difficult, or will take a good deal of time, if (for whatever reason) you can't do everything now that you think should be done, you should do whatever *can* be done. Whatever you do will make you that much safer.

One way to start is by buying some gold coins, so that at least you have something you can hold in your hands and call your own. Transferring money from your bank into a money market fund invested in Treasury securities is another good way to remove some of your vulnerability quickly.

If your portfolio now is dominated by one investment—whether it be stocks, municipal bonds, gold, a bank account, real-estate holdings, whatever—sell some of it and use the proceeds to purchase a Permanent Portfolio investment you don't already have.

If you're having trouble getting started, consider using whatever liquid capital you have to open an account with the Permanent Portfolio Fund. That's a mutual fund that was created in 1982 by my colleague Terry Coxon to implement the Permanent Portfolio concept. Details of the fund are given on pages 242–243. You can write one check and immediately obtain the coverage a Permanent Portfolio is meant to provide. That will take the pressure off while you're working out your own Permanent Portfolio.

The important thing is to do something. After the first step, the second won't seem so difficult.

Of course, you may find that even the first step is easy—that nothing stands between you and a safe Permanent Portfolio. If so, you can be insulated, safe and sound, by this time next week.

20

Where to Get Help

This chapter describes some products, services, and companies that may help you construct and manage a Permanent Portfolio. Many of them also can be useful for a Variable Portfolio. Included are investment dealers and brokers, mutual funds, and other sources of help.

Obviously, you don't need all the services you'll find here. You may not want any of them. I've included this material in case you don't know where to find something you need, and also because I've found some of the companies or services to be particularly appropriate for the Permanent Portfolio concept.

As you read through the chapter, mark anything that catches your eye. When you've finished the book, call or write for information from the sources you've marked. After you've examined the material they send, you can decide whether you want to do business with them.

There undoubtedly are many useful sources that aren't listed here. I've included only those with which I have some acquaintance or that are known nationally.

There are a few products and services that I've tried to get onto the market to make it easier for investors to use my Permanent

Portfolio concept. I've done this either by encouraging others to develop something or by becoming directly involved myself. So I'm associated with some of the products listed in this chapter, and I hope you won't find that irritating. Where I haven't indicated that I'm involved, I have no financial interest—except perhaps as a customer.

Needless to say, other than for my own services, I don't control what anyone does. So I can't guarantee the terms of your relationship with any company mentioned here. You'll have to evaluate each of them as you would a perfect (or imperfect) stranger. They're listed here not as recommendations, but to save you having to hunt for them.

STOCK MARKET MUTUAL FUNDS

As discussed on pages 171–172, most investors will find mutual funds the easiest way to diversify the Permanent Portfolio's stock-market holdings.

Each of the seven funds listed here is highly volatile, remains fully invested in stocks as a stated policy, has no sales or redemption fees, and is available in most states. All offer IRAs and Keogh plans.

Before selecting these seven, I investigated several hundred funds. Any other funds that meet my standards weren't operating when I made my selections.

Columbia Growth Fund
1301 S.W. Fifth
P.O. Box 1350
Portland, Oregon 97207
(503) 222-3600
(800) 547-1037
Minimum investment: $1,000

The Evergreen Fund, Inc.
550 Mamaroneck Avenue
Harrison, New York 10528
(914) 698-5711
(800) 235-0064
Minimum investment: $2,000

Manhattan Fund, Inc.
Neuberger & Berman
  Management, Inc.
342 Madison Avenue
New York, New York 10173
(212) 850-8300, (800) 367-0770
Minimum investment: $1,000

W. L. Morgan Growth Fund
Vanguard Financial Center
P.O. Box 2600
Valley Forge, Pennsylvania
  19482
(215) 648-6000
(800) 662-7447
Minimum investment: $1,500

Scudder Capital Growth
  Fund, Inc.
160 Federal Street
Boston, Massachusetts 02110
(617) 439-4640, (800) 225-2470
Minimum investment: $1,000

Tudor Fund
One New York Plaza
New York, New York 10004
(212) 908-9582
(800) 223-3332
Minimum investment: $1,000

Twentieth Century Growth
  Investors
P.O. Box 419200
Kansas City, Missouri 64141
(816) 531-5575
(800) 345-2021
Minimum investment: None

Daily prices for these funds are listed in the "Mutual Funds" table in the financial section of most daily newspapers. Manhattan Fund is listed under "Neuberger Berman"; Tudor is listed under "Weiss Peck Greer"; and W. L. Morgan is listed under "Vanguard Group."

Write or call each fund that interests you to obtain information and a prospectus that describes the fund in detail.

Mutual Fund Information

Two annual directories contain extensive information about hundreds of mutual funds. If you hear of a fund, you might want to consult one of the directories to see whether the fund is appropriate for the Permanent Portfolio.

The Handbook for No-Load Fund Investors, P.O. Box 283, Hastings-on-Hudson, New York 10706; $38. This is a cardcover, letter-sized, 400-page directory of no-load and low-load mutual funds (funds with no commissions or small commissions). The directory shows performance records going back 10 years, as well as the funds' betas (volatility) and information concerning their investment policies. Also included are articles explaining the mechanics of investing in mutual funds.

Wiesenberger Investment Companies Service, 210 South Street, Boston, Massachusetts 02111; $375 per year. This service is expensive, but it is by far the most thorough coverage of the industry. If you need to consult it only once, you might look for it in a large library. It is an annual, oversized, 900-page, hardcover book that contains information on virtually every U.S. mutual fund (both load and no-load) and closed-end investment company. Performance records go back 25 years, and most funds are described in detail—history, policies, annual yields, size, and so on. There are tables comparing volatility. The $375 price also includes two monthly newsletters about mutual funds.

U.S. TREASURY SECURITIES

To find what maturities of Treasury bills, notes, or bonds are currently available, you need only look in the financial section of a daily newspaper under "Treasury Securities" or a similar heading.

You can buy Treasury bills or bonds from stockbrokers, Swiss banks, and most U.S. banks. Six national brokerage companies are listed on page 242, and three Swiss banks are listed on page 239.

If, for any reason, you want to understand these instruments better, here are two books that do a good job of explaining the government securities markets.

The Money Market: Myth, Reality, and Practice, by Marcia Stigum, tells you virtually everything you could ever want to know about the buying and selling of short-term dollar instruments—

Treasury bills, CDs, commercial paper, Eurodollars, banker's acceptances, repurchase agreements ("repos"), and on and on and on. It even includes detailed explanations of the futures markets for these instruments.

Although some of the topics aren't easy to grasp at a first reading, the author does the best job possible to make the material understandable. Published in 1978 (and revised in 1983) by Dow Jones-Irwin, Homewood, Illinois 60430; $47.50.

The Complete Bond Book, by David M. Darst, explains interest yields, bonds, and the works right from the beginning. It assumes much less knowledge on the part of the reader than the book by Marcia Stigum (above) does. And yet Mr. Darst's book introduces a great many advanced concepts as well. It covers both short-term and long-term fixed-interest securities. Published in 1975 by McGraw-Hill, Inc., P.O. Box 402, Heightstown, New Jersey 08520; $44.95.

GOLD

Information on buying gold from U.S. dealers appears on page 175. You also can buy gold through a Swiss bank, as discussed on pages 206–207. Three Swiss banks are listed on page 239.

Under "Coin Dealers" in the Yellow Pages, you can find a local dealer that sells low-premium gold coins such as Canadian Maple Leafs, Krugerrands, and American Eagles, as well as "junk" silver coins minted by the U.S. government before 1965.

The companies listed here sell nationwide by mail and telephone, and will ship anywhere you designate.

Benham Certified Metals
755 Page Mill Road
Palo Alto, California 94304
(800) 447-4653
(415) 858-3607

Blanchard & Co., Inc.
2400 Jefferson Highway
Jefferson, Louisiana 70121
(800) 877-7633
(504) 837-3010

Camino Coin Co.
P.O. Box 4292
Burlingame, California 94010
(800) 348-8001
(415) 348-3000

Guardian Trust Co.
123 Yonge Street
Toronto, Ontario M5C 1S8
Canada
(800) 268-9556
(416) 863-1100

Investment Rarities
One Appletree Square
Suite 1500
Minneapolis, Minnesota
   55420
(800) 328-1860
(612) 853-0700

Monex International Ltd.
4910 Birch Street
Newport Beach, California
   92660
(800) 854-3361
(714) 752-1400

Numisco Inc.
141 West Jackson
Chicago, Illinois 60604
(800) 621-1339
(312) 427-0600

Gold Storage

These banks store gold for individual customers, as well as for gold dealers.

Bank of Delaware
519 North Market Street
Wilmington, Delaware
   19801
Attn: Precious Metals
   Storage
(302) 429-2144

Chase Manhattan Bank N.A.
Precious Metals Vault
   Service
1 Chase Manhattan Plaza, 2B
18th Floor
New York, New York 10081
(212) 552-1327

Citibank N.A.
399 Park Avenue, Level C
New York, New York 10043
Attn: Precious Metals
 Services
(212) 559-3630

Iron Mountain Depository
 Corp.
26 Broadway
New York, New York 10004
Attn: Precious Metals
 Storage
(212) 912-8531

Republic National Bank of
 New York
452 Fifth Avenue
New York, New York
 10018
Attn: Precious Metals
 Storage
(212) 930-6439

Rhode Island Hospital Trust
 National Bank
Precious Metals Department
15 Westminster Street
Suite 915
Providence, Rhode Island
 02903
(401) 278-8000
(800) 343-8419

Swiss Bank Corporation
P.O. Box 395
Church Street Station
New York, New York
 10008
Attn: Bullion Vault
(212) 574-3644

Wilmington Trust Company
Rodney Square North
Wilmington, Delaware
 19890
Attn: Precious Metals
(302) 651-1000

Gold Trust

The United States Gold Trust is a trust (similar to a mutual fund) that is 100% invested in gold bullion and American Eagle gold coins at all times. The trust's gold is stored with a U.S. bank custodian.

Investing through the Gold Trust has several advantages. You get the convenience of mutual-fund investing, you don't have to bother handling the gold, transaction costs are lower than for most gold investments, and you can buy or sell the exact dollar amount you want at any time.

For the Permanent Portfolio, the trust is attractive in two ways. One is that it provides an easy way to get started with a gold investment, before you've made other arrangements for gold storage. And, second, with some part of your Permanent Portfolio gold budget in the trust, you have a convenient place to make portfolio adjustments to the penny. (The minimum investment is $2,000.)

If you are familiar with mutual-fund investing, you probably will find the Gold Trust very attractive. Nevertheless, I hope you'll go to the trouble of buying and storing at least some Permanent Portfolio gold on your own.

The trust also is a convenient medium for Variable Portfolio investments—since you don't have to be concerned with handling the gold, and you can buy the exact dollar amount that fits your purpose.

I am a limited partner in, and consultant to, World Money Managers, which owns the United States Gold Trust's sponsor.

To obtain further information, contact:

> The United States Gold Trust
> Investor's Information Office
> 207 Jefferson Square
> Austin, Texas 78731
> (512) 453-7558, (800) 531-5142

SWISS BANKS

Here are three Swiss banks with which I've had dealings for many years. All three are very liquid, provide good service to English-speaking customers, and will purchase and hold gold coins for you in any quantity.

Anker Bank SA[1]
50 Avenue de la Gare
P.O. Box 159
CH-1001 Lausanne, Switzerland
Telephone: (21) 20-4741
Contact: Mrs. Francine Misrahi or Jean Gander
Minimum to open account: $5,000
Assets SF 185 million; liquidity 76%.

Cambio + Valorenbank
Utoquai 55, P.O. Box 535
CH-8021 Zürich, Switzerland
Telephone: (1) 252-2000
Contact: Werner W. Schwarz or Hans Bachmann
Minimum to open account: $50,000
Assets SF 115 million; liquidity 83%.

Foreign Commerce Bank
Bellariastrasse 82
CH-8038 Zürich, Switzerland
Telephone: (1) 482-6688
Contact: Bruno Brodbeck, Peter Weber, or Roger Badet
Minimum to open account: $10,000
Assets SF 328 million; liquidity 78%.

Foreign Commerce Bank has a representative office at:
P.O. Box 91717
West Vancouver, British Columbia, Canada V7V 3P2
Telephone: (604) 925-3551
Contact: Adrian Hartmann

Asset figures and liquidity ratings for Anker Bank are as of
January 1988. Figures for the others are as of June 1988. The
liquidity rating is my own calculation of how well a bank matches

---

[1]Formerly Banque Indiana and Banque Ankerfina.

its maturities; all three banks' ratings are well above the average for Swiss banks.

MONEY MARKET FUNDS

Here are three money market funds that invest only in Treasury bills. Because these funds are extremely safety-conscious, they don't invest in repurchase agreements (which are short-term loans secured by U.S. Treasury securities). Nor do they invest in notes issued by government agencies other than the U.S. Treasury itself. They are particularly appropriate for the cash budget of the Permanent Portfolio.

Capital Preservation Fund
755 Page Mill Road
Palo Alto, California 94304
(415) 858-3609
(800) 227-8380
Minimum investment: $1,000

Treasury Bill Portfolio
Box 5847
Austin, Texas 78763
(512) 453-7558
(800) 531-5142
Minimum investment: $1,000

Neuberger & Berman
  Government Money Fund,
  Inc.
342 Madison Avenue
New York, New York 10173
(212) 850-8300
(800) 367-0770
Minimum investment: $2,000

All three funds allow redemption by check. The Treasury Bill Portfolio, unlike most money market funds, adds part of its income to the redemption value of its shares—rather than paying it all out in taxable dividends. This policy causes the share price to rise, and defers part of the shareholder's tax liability until his shares are sold.[2]

[2]I am a limited partner in, and a consultant to, the Treasury Bill Portfolio's investment advisor.

ONE-STOP BROKERS

Many stockbrokers have expanded their services in recent years, so that they now offer most of the investments you might want for a Permanent Portfolio or a Variable Portfolio. For our purposes, these include common stocks, Treasury bonds, Treasury bills, and even American Eagle gold coins in many cases.

A stockbroker also can help you set up an IRA or Keogh plan if you're eligible for one.

Stockbrokers sell mutual funds, too. However, their funds all have sales commissions that, in my opinion, are prohibitive. I prefer to buy no-load mutual funds directly from the funds themselves. Seven such funds are listed on pages 232–233.

Most major brokerage companies also offer money market funds. I believe it's very important that the Permanent Portfolio cash budget stay in a money market fund that invests *exclusively* in Treasury securities. If the stockbroker you deal with has such a fund, fine. But I'm not aware of any that do.

A brokerage account is a convenient location for a Variable Portfolio. With a phone call, you can switch your money from one investment to another among stocks, bonds, gold coins, gold stocks, commodity futures, and much else.

If you already deal with a stockbroker, tell him which services you need. If he can't be of enough help to you, try the large national companies.

You can check the telephone book for the local phone numbers of national firms. Or you can write or call the offices listed below for information. All these firms do business by telephone and mail, in addition to having local offices throughout the United States. All except Charles Schwab handle gold coins.[3]

---

[3]Charles Schwab also provides a convenient service for purchasing certain no-load mutual funds. This isn't appropriate for the Permanent Portfolio, since it places someone between you and your investments. But it's a convenient way to invest in no-load mutual funds for the Variable Portfolio.

Dean Witter Reynolds, Inc.
801 Brickell Avenue
20th Floor, #60
Miami, Florida 33131
(305) 347-6754

Prudential Bache Securities
One Seaport Plaza
199 Water Street
New York, New York 10292
(212) 214-1000

Merrill Lynch, Pierce,
  Fenner & Smith, Inc.
250 Vesey Street
New York, New York
  10281
(800) 637-7455

Charles Schwab & Co., Inc.
101 Montgomery Street
San Francisco, California
  94104
(415) 627-7000
(800) 648-5300

PaineWebber Group, Inc.
1285 Avenue of the
  Americas
New York, New York
  10019
(212) 713-2000

Shearson Lehman
  Hutton, Inc.
World Financial Center
American Express Tower C
New York, New York 10285
(212) 298-2000

HELP IN CREATING A PERMANENT PORTFOLIO

The services in this section are designed to provide help in creating a Permanent Portfolio.

Permanent Portfolio Fund

The Permanent Portfolio Fund is a no-load mutual fund created specifically to carry out the Permanent Portfolio concept. I am a consultant to the fund, as well as a limited partner in the company that manages the fund.

Because the Permanent Portfolio Fund is able to achieve greater diversification than the average investor could achieve on his own, it includes more investments than those I've suggested in this book. The fund maintains fixed percentages for those investments, never attempting to outguess the markets. The minimum investment is $1,000.

The fund was created in 1982 by Terry Coxon, who has been my associate since 1974. During its years of operation, the fund has performed as you would expect a Permanent Portfolio to perform—rising in value whenever at least one major investment is in a bull market.

The fund is a way to establish an instant Permanent Portfolio, perhaps while deciding how to go about setting up one on your own.

Even if you do construct your own Permanent Portfolio, you may want to put part of your capital into the fund for additional diversification, to have a convenient way to add or withdraw money from your own Permanent Portfolio without disturbing its percentages, or simply so that you can receive communications from the fund that discuss the Permanent Portfolio concept. The fund also can retain part of its profits to share value which reduces your yearly tax liability.

You can obtain a prospectus and brochure from the Permanent Portfolio Fund, P.O. Box 5847, Austin, Texas 78763; (800) 531-5142, (512) 453-7558.

Personal Consulting

Terry Coxon, president of the Permanent Portfolio Fund, also provides an individual advisory service to help investors design, establish, and maintain a Permanent Portfolio for themselves.

He is well versed in a wide range of financial matters—including tax planning, the use of foreign banks and other foreign institutions, and the creation of hedges to offset illiquid investments. Some of the ideas in this book were developed by him in the course of assisting clients and in establishing the Permanent Portfolio Fund. He edited this book and edits every issue of my newsletter.

You can contact him at Private Investors, 7 Fourth Street, Suite 14, Petaluma, California 94952; (707) 762-5336.

Computer Program

The Dual Portfolio Manager is a computer program that was designed specifically to help in managing a Permanent Portfolio. I wasn't involved in developing it, but I believe it's a useful tool for anyone with a personal computer.

The program implements the investment strategy presented in this book. It allows you to use my four-essential-investments approach, or to include any investments you want.

The program identifies the purchases and sales needed for annual portfolio adjustments, provides helpful tools for operating a Variable Portfolio, calculates the tax consequences of investment sales, and tells you just about anything you need to know about either portfolio. The program comes with detailed, step-by-step instructions—and makes all the bookkeeping chores relatively easy.

The program costs $99 and runs on any IBM-compatible personal computer. It is available from C. R. Hunter & Associates, Inc., 1176 Inner Circle, Cincinnati, Ohio 45240; (513) 825-8669.

MY SERVICES

When I wrote *The Economic Time Bomb,* I felt it was important for the book to be reasonably short. I wanted it to be approachable—something you could go through in an evening. I didn't want you to put off reading it until your next three-week vacation.

For most people, everything needed to get started with a Permanent Portfolio can be found in Part II. But you may still have questions or require further help, perhaps because of special circumstances. Or you may want more ideas about Variable Portfolio investments. So this section discusses other services I offer.

The Best-Laid Plans

Why the Best-Laid Investment Plans Usually Go Wrong, published in 1987, is a 544-page book that devotes over 200 pages to everything I could think of that might be encountered in implementing the Permanent and Variable Portfolios.

It covers a great many details concerning the buying of mutual funds, Treasury bonds, and gold; has a chapter devoted to Swiss banks; and contains a detailed explanation of the strategy I use for my Variable Portfolio.

The book also attempts to provide a realistic look at fundamental and technical analysis, other market systems, forecasting, advisory records, and the many get-rich schemes promoted to investors.

Any bookstore should have it or be willing to order it for you. The hardcover edition is $19.95; a cardcover edition is $12.95. If you have trouble locating the book, you can order it through my office: Box 5586, Austin, Texas 78763; (512) 453-7313, (800) 531-5142.

Harry Browne's Special Reports

My newsletter discusses the Permanent Portfolio strategy—describing techniques and new investment products that can make the strategy more effective or easier to apply.

The newsletter provides regular updates to this book—watching the money supply, the FDIC, bank problems, the government budget, the development of dangerous non-problems, and other factors that might speed up or set off the economic time bomb.

And there are concrete suggestions for Variable Portfolio

speculations whenever I see a low-risk opportunity for a large profit.

A typical issue runs 20 to 30 pages—including comments on the investment markets, the economy, and current events; feature articles on investment strategy; graphs; and answers to questions from subscribers.

The letter isn't published on a calendar schedule. Instead, an issue is sent whenever I believe I have something useful to say—which usually turns out to be every 4 to 6 weeks. A subscription is for the next 10 issues and costs $225. You can purchase the current issue (once, as a sample) for $5 from *Harry Browne's Special Reports,* Box 5586A, Austin, Texas 78763; (800) 531-5142, (512) 453-7313.

Consulting & Investment Management

I also provide a consultation-by-mail service to help individuals set up a Permanent Portfolio. And I manage Variable Portfolios on a continuing basis. If either of these services interests you, you can get more details by contacting the newsletter office shown above.

ECONOMIC DATA

A Permanent Portfolio removes the need to be alert to everything that goes on in the world. But if you want a convenient source of up-to-date economic data—either out of curiosity or to help with your Variable Portfolio—the following three publications are inexpensive sources of the economic statistics that interest most investors.

Economic Indicators

This 38-page booklet, published monthly by the U.S. Department of Commerce, provides statistics and graphs for major economic indicators—such as Gross National Product, employment, prices, money supply, government finance, and interest rates. Most tables show monthly data for the past 12 months and yearly data for the past 8 years. The graphs cover 5 to 8 years. It is an ideal source for a quick update of major statistics.

Economic Indicators, Superintendent of Documents, Government Printing Office, Washington, D.C. 20402; $27 per year, $2.50 for one issue.

Federal Reserve Bulletin

This monthly publication is more detailed than *Economic Indicators.* Each issue includes about 75 pages of tables on the U.S. economy and financial markets. Most tables show monthly data for the latest 6 months and annual data for the last 3 years.

Federal Reserve Bulletin, Publications Services, Board of Governors of the Federal Reserve System, Washington, D.C. 20551; $20 per year, $2 per issue.

International Financial Statistics

This monthly, 500-page statistical summary, published by the International Monetary Fund, is the best source I've found for data on foreign countries.

For each of more than 100 countries, the most important economic indicators are provided—including money supply, exchange rates, gold holdings, prices, interest rates, and many others. Figures are shown for the latest 7 to 10 months, 13 to 16 quarters, and 7 years. A yearbook (included in the subscription price) provides annual data going back 30 years or so.

International Financial Statistics, International Monetary Fund, Washington, D.C. 20431; $100 per year, $10 for a single issue, or $25 for the yearbook alone.

INVESTING MECHANICS

I've never found a book that thoroughly explains the basics of each type of investment—written with the assumption that the reader knows nothing at all about the investment at hand. Such a book may exist, but I've yet to see it.

In the meantime, the next best thing is *Barron's Finance and Investment Handbook*—an excellent reference work by John Downes and Jordan Elliot Goodman. It contains a wealth of information about almost every kind of investment. The heart of the book is a 383-page dictionary of economic and financial terms—most of which are explained in everyday language.

The entire hardcover book is 994 pages. There are sections explaining how to read the price tables in a newspaper's financial section, giving yearly historical data for many indices and economic indicators, listing mutual funds, explaining the minute details of futures contracts, showing how to read an annual report, and on and on.

The book may be available from your local bookstore, or you can order it from Barron's Educational Series, Inc., 250 Wireless Boulevard, Hauppauge, New York 11788; $21.95.

21

Ready for Anything

In Chapter 12, I said your investment strategy should satisfy six requirements. We can review those requirements now, to see how the strategy we've discussed measures up to them.

Checklist

1. *Your investment program must do well in any economic climate.*

The Permanent Portfolio will take care of you whether the future holds prosperity, inflation, tight money, recession, deflation, depression, a stock market crash, or anything else. Through careful balance, it assures that at least one of its investments will carry the portfolio in any economic climate.

2. *Your investments must do well without your having to foresee changes in the economic climate.*

Because a Permanent Portfolio is *permanent,* you don't have to know what's coming next. You don't have to put your wealth and savings and life into the hands of a financial fortune-teller who claims he can see into the future. You don't have to wonder which of the contradictory "expert" opinions you hear is the right one.

3. *You shouldn't have to change your investments as the climate changes.*

Because the Permanent Portfolio is ready for anything, you don't have to tinker with it, reevaluate it, worry that maybe you should be doing something different, or wonder whether it can deal with the latest threat to come to your attention.

4. *Your investment program must be tough enough to tolerate all surprises.*

With the Permanent Portfolio, you're prepared for any surprise. For example, on October 19, 1987, the Dow Jones Industrial Average fell 22% in 6½ hours; the four-investment Permanent Portfolio fell 4%. A shocking, totally unexpected blow that injured most investment programs left the Permanent Portfolio with barely a scratch.

Look again at the graph on page 158. The line representing the stock market looks like Niagara Falls in the middle of 1987—as the stock market drops almost vertically. As if that weren't enough, notice the line representing bonds; during 1987 it drops as much as the stock market, although more slowly.

Now look at the line representing the Permanent Portfolio; it sometimes jiggles, but it never plunges. Catastrophes in individual investments register only as little blips in the Permanent Portfolio's inexorable upward path.

For investors with a Permanent Portfolio, the stock market crash was a spectacle—not a personal disaster.

5. *You must be able to "walk away" from your investments— confident that they are taking care of you, no matter what happens.*

Because you know the Permanent Portfolio can survive any surprise, and because it doesn't have to be reexamined in the light of current events, you truly can ignore your investments. You no longer have to worry about them, monitor them, or be troubled by them.

For once in your life, you can turn your attention to the things that you care about with no fear that you're leaving your savings and wealth unprotected.

6. *You must be able to bet on the future, if you want to, without risking any capital that's precious to you.*

The Variable Portfolio is there to satisfy any speculative urge you might have. If you judge that some particular event is likely—something that will affect an investment in a big way—you can bet on your judgment with the Variable Portfolio.

You can place your bet freely and enthusiastically—knowing that you aren't risking anything that's precious to you, knowing that the Permanent Portfolio is a safety net under your trapeze act.

SURPRISES

It is in the realm of surprises that the Permanent Portfolio provides its most dramatic benefit.

One characteristic of human nature is the invincible belief that one will be able, somehow, to handle whatever comes. It's easy to think that you'll adjust and deal with changing trends, new developments, or whatever. And perhaps you will—if they don't rush at you suddenly.

But sometimes they do. You can't prepare for the sudden, catastrophic disaster that occurred yesterday. The most you can do is pick up the pieces.

And life is full of these bolts from the blue—sudden, totally unexpected events that turn your world upside down.

If you have a heart attack, you can change your diet, lower your blood pressure, and exercise more. But you can't undo what happened—the pain, the weeks lost, and perhaps the permanent physical damage.

If you have a car accident because your brakes failed, you can't heal an injury by arranging for more frequent maintenance in the future.

You can avoid only the dangers you've prepared for in advance.

Unfortunately, there are so many things in life that you're

supposed to be preparing for. You're bombarded continually with news about more and more threats. Defending against all of them would take up most of your day. By the time you've finished jogging, flossing, studying food labels, meditating, inspecting your car, checking the evening news, praying, and having an encounter-therapy dialogue with your family, it's already time for bed.

How nice it is to know there's one area of your life you don't have to worry about anymore. Once you have a Permanent Port-folio in place, you at least can forget about your money and investments—and devote more time to perfecting your tofu ham-burgers.

Sudden Changes

In the fall of 1987, many people suspected they were overinvested in the stock market. Perhaps they thought they would sell some of their stocks if the market went much lower.

Then one day, in a matter of a few hours, it was too late. Suddenly life had turned upside down for someone who had to accept the disappearance of a quarter of his life savings.

And yet, that misfortune was comparatively mild.

How many times have you heard about people who lost *every-thing* because all their savings were in an uninsured bank or thrift institution that failed? Perhaps you'd never be so foolish as to put all your money in an uninsured bank. But how do you know that FDIC insurance is safe? Did you ever study the FDIC's financial statement to verify that it really can back up your bank deposit?

Surprises don't discriminate. People who were very wealthy have become poor overnight when they found out that their money had been stolen or squandered by the money-management genius who had put them in all the right investments, sheltered away all taxes, and relieved them of all need to think about their finances.

There are crowds of people in Texas whose heads were never turned by any investment fad, or by bull markets in stocks and gold. They kept their capital in real estate, "conservatively" leveraged—only to see their wealth disappear when oil prices plunged and the Texas economy came apart.

We could go on for pages with examples of people who put all their faith in municipal bonds, or their own business, or art objects, or some other safe haven—only to see it all disappear because of one sudden, unforeseen event.

The only way to be protected against such a surprise is with a balanced, diversified portfolio that isn't vulnerable to sudden shocks.

With a Permanent Portfolio, that's what you'll have. You'll survive surprises that would be catastrophic for others—and you won't be left behind if the surprise of the 1990s is prosperity.

WHAT CAN HURT YOU?

You still will encounter opinions, theories, and warnings about investments. And, at first, they may make you wonder whether you should change something in your Permanent Portfolio. But no matter what the notion, if you take a moment to think it through, you'll realize you're covered already.

Even if the event would be bad for one of the investments in the Permanent Portfolio, it probably would be good for another one. If you alter the portfolio to respond to the latest threat or opportunity, you'll throw it out of balance and leave yourself exposed to other events that might surprise you.

By staying with the Permanent Portfolio, you'll *always* be holding the most appropriate investment protection. Eventually, this fact will sink in—and then you'll easily resist temptations to tinker with your protection.

Shortly after the 1987 stock market crash, I received a letter containing this paragraph:

On the day the market slumped 500 points, our son was visiting from college. He was amazed that we took the event with equanimity. We explained to him the theory of the Permanent Portfolio and how it can bring peace of mind.

Very soon you'll have the same serenity. Then you can relax completely and let the rest of the world go by.

Epilogue

22

Confessions of Mr. X

In April 1970, my first book, *How You Can Profit from the Coming Devaluation,* was published. It maintained that bad times were coming, and it advised investors to get rid of stocks and bonds—and buy gold, silver, and Swiss francs instead. The book sold far better than I had expected, and many people acted on my advice.

During the next few years, the economy did indeed begin to suffer. Inflation heated up; the stock market had its worst years since the early 1930s; and gold, silver, and the Swiss franc all moved sharply upward in price.

As a result, my 1974 book, *You Can Profit from a Monetary Crisis,* was an even bigger hit, reaching #1 on the best-seller lists. I had become a celebrity in the investment world, and my views were quoted widely.

The recommended investments continued to go up. By 1980, gold had risen to $850 from $35 in 1970, silver to $48 from $2, and the Swiss franc to $.67 from $.23. Of course, those were their peaks, and they came down sharply afterward.

But I achieved a second coup: I advised selling each investment near its highest price. My 1978 book, *New Profits from the Monetary Crisis,* said that the Swiss franc had probably gone about as

high as it was going to—and the book was released the very month
the franc peaked. I published "Farewell to Silver" in my newsletter in January 1980, when silver was at $38—two weeks before its
peak. And my newsletter exited its Variable Portfolio positions in
gold in the spring of 1980, when two stop-losses were triggered at
an average price of $585.[1]

I know of no one else who recommended gold, silver, and Swiss
francs in the early 1970s, stayed with them faithfully throughout
the 1970s, and then advised selling them near their peaks at the
end of the decade.

The Precious Secret

You might want to know the secret of my success. And if you
don't, I'll tell you anyway: *I was lucky.*

I don't mean blind, dumb luck—like winning a lottery. I do
mean that, despite my best effort to identify the best investments,
events could easily have gone against me. In retrospect I can see
what I didn't see then: the investments I was so sure of could easily
have turned out to be losers.

As it was, investors who followed my advice had to wait out
uncomfortable declines in the three investments in the mid-1970s.
And many of my expectations for the 1970s didn't come to pass.
Fortunately, though, enough of them did pan out to create enormous profits.

I'm sure you've heard, at one time or another, of a legendary
financial genius who made fortunes for himself and others through
his uncanny investment insights—buying and selling at just the
right times.

Well, now you're reading the words of one such legendary
figure. Probably no one in the world made more money for more
investors in the 1970s than I did. Certainly, no one else recom-

---

[1] A stop-loss is an instruction to a broker or dealer to sell one's holdings automatically if
the price drops to a specified level.

mended gold, silver, and the Swiss franc steadfastly throughout the decade, and then recommended selling—only once—in time to keep most of the profits.

But the "genius" can tell you this: If I hadn't been lucky, the world would never have had reason to notice me. By now I might be Henry Kaufman's chauffeur instead.

Luck isn't everything. It's not even the most important thing; the right strategy will capitalize on good luck and soften the effects of bad luck. But luck is always a factor, and sensational results are impossible without sensationally good luck.

If you're trying to outguess the markets, it isn't enough to be smart or thorough or talented; fortune must smile on you. And even if it does, one's luck is sure to change eventually. Remember this when you're asked to bet your life savings on an advisor who predicted the stock market crash or who boasts of having slain some other dragon.

Revelations

In my case, it wasn't too long before I recognized how lucky I had been.

I began my investment newsletter in December 1974. Since January was traditionally the time to make forecasts, I set to work preparing my 1975 predictions for the economy, interest rates, the stock market, gold, and other matters.

I was sure I could provide perceptive insights for my readers. After all, hadn't I successfully predicted the devaluation of the dollar and the runaway rise in gold and silver? I was a proven forecaster.

I worked very hard on those forecasts. I examined a great deal of data, and I gave considerable thought to the possibilities for the coming year. When I knew exactly what was going to happen in 1975, I published my forecasts in the newsletter.

And then I began praying they would come true.

When I realized that I had to hope for the right outcome—that, no matter how careful I was, I still had to be lucky—I knew I had to find a better way.

A Better Way

Over time, I became more uneasy with a reputation as a seer and with the thought of relying on forecasts for protection. No matter how sure I was that my overall vision of the future was correct, events too often wandered from my script.

Eventually, I found a way to deemphasize forecasting. I first presented the new approach in 1977 in my newsletter, and in 1978 in my book *New Profits from the Monetary Crisis.*

The first step was to separate one's capital into two portfolios— the Permanent and Variable Portfolios—as I've discussed in this book.

The second step was to make the Permanent Portfolio less dependent on one future. I suggested that readers reduce their reliance on gold, silver, and the Swiss franc, and add stocks and cash—to provide a source of profit in periods of low inflation.

My colleague, Terry Coxon, had been urging this move toward balance since we began working together in 1974. Between 1978 and 1981, he and I collaborated to enhance the safety and balance of the Permanent Portfolio. We published our ideas in *Inflation-Proofing Your Investments* in 1981.

In 1987, *Why the Best-Laid Investment Plans Usually Go Wrong* refined the strategy further, with the simpler approach that's also in this book.

The strategy worked well from its inception in 1977. Every refinement has been only to enhance its balance, safety, and simplicity.

The Permanent Portfolio did its job in the inflationary turmoil of the late 1970s, the tight-money recessions of the early 1980s, the stock and bond bull markets of the mid-1980s, and the stock market crash of 1987.

Now I feel no need to foresee the future and no fear that luck may leave me, because I know I can be safe no matter what happens.

MR. X

But even if *I* am reduced to hoping when making forecasts, maybe there's someone somewhere who doesn't need to hope—someone who *knows* what's going to happen next.

If you pay much attention to the world of investing, you're bound to have heard of someone like that—a savvy genius with an amazing track record, who has announced the start and end of every bull market with perfect timing, and who's always on the right side of the market. Since I don't know his name, I'll refer to him as Mr. X.

Think about Mr. X for a moment. Let the implications of his existence sink in. Here is someone who's always right about the future of investments.

If Mr. X exists, what need do we have for anyone else?

If Mr. X can do what you've been told he can do, why then would Louis Rukeyser or 'Adam Smith' or Henry Kaufman or Andrew Tobias or Howard Ruff or Martin Zweig or I or anyone else waste his time pondering the investment markets?

I could pay for Mr. X's analysis and simply recommend whatever he recommends. I'd be right every time. How much more attractive and dramatic that would be than talking about the ho-hum, eat-your-vegetables Permanent Portfolio.

Why don't I simply relay Mr. X's insights? Because he doesn't exist. I've read hundreds of investment books. I've met scores of investment experts. And I've read more investment newsletters than I care to count. If Mr. X existed, he wouldn't have escaped my notice.

Of course, there are thousands of Mr. X impersonators out there. Some of them have secret contacts inside the Federal Reserve or the highest levels of government; some have developed systems that have been proven to work in every bull and bear market; others have invented "proprietary indicators" that are invariably right about the course of the market.

Some of them foretold the 1987 stock market crash, others were the first to buy the day after the crash, others picked the exact high for gold or stocks or interest rates 18 months in advance. All these wonderful achievements were clearcut, unambiguous, decisive, and unbelievably profitable.

But no matter how rock-solid and infallible these people are at a distance, they never live up to their reputations when you get close.

You begin following the advice of one of them, avidly waiting for his next landmark prediction. You're excited because you'll be the first on your block to know of the next great investment opportunity.

But nothing happens. A gain here, a loss there, a loss here, a gain there. Right occasionally, wrong just as often.

You thought you'd found Mr. X, but he turned out to be Mr. Z.

Mr. Z is right from time to time—just as *you* would be if you published forecasts and investment advice. But time to time isn't often enough. One bad forecast can undo the gains earned by many correct recommendations.

It may not be welcome news, but there is no Mr. X. No one can predict the future. If anyone could, we'd *all* be billionaires by now, because—one way or another—Mr. X's predictions would become known to us.

And when a would-be Mr. X shows you his performance record, remember that at one time my record could have led people to think that *I* was Mr. X. And you know why I succeeded.

WHAT IF I'M WRONG?

By now I must have made it clear that Part I wasn't a prophecy, a road map, or a timetable. It was an attempt to show where the future could lead us, and to prod you to protect yourself from the economic time bomb.

But what if the economic time bomb never explodes?

Suppose we look back in 1995 and see that America has suffered nothing worse than one or two mild recessions and an inflation rate that peaked at 8%. Even if the federal debt has risen tenfold, maybe interest rates will still be around 8% to 10%. And although bank failures might still be in the news, perhaps the FDIC is continuing to keep the mess cleaned up—just as President Jackson has promised it would.[2]

What then?

Will you be sorry you read this book? Will you regret having heard about those silly Portfolios with their capital "P"s? Will you feel you've spent the intervening 6 years in a financial bomb shelter, while your friends were getting rich?

I don't see how.

In the first place, you'll have spent 6 worry-free years—while most people will have suffered great anxiety about their savings and investments. Your lower blood pressure ought to count for something.

You'll have been freer to enjoy life than others were. You also will have been freer to speculate if you wanted to, because you knew a safety net was spread beneath you.

Although the Permanent Portfolio gives you the security of an insurance policy, it's better than insurance—because a Permanent Portfolio doesn't cost you anything. Safety doesn't come at the expense of growth. In fact, you may earn a better return on your Permanent Portfolio, year after year, than you've ever enjoyed on your investments.

[2]As he said in his State Of The Union message on January 15, 1995:
"The future of banks is sunny.
So don't withdraw your money."

It's true that someone's investments will outperform your Permanent Portfolio this year. And someone's investments will outperform your portfolio next year. You may never have a year in which you're #1. But, most likely, each year it will be a different group of people who outperform you. Over several years, very few will outperform your Permanent Portfolio.

And if you doubt that, use your Variable Portfolio to become #1.

I hope you make it.

HOPING TO BE WRONG

It's common in crisis books for the author to say something like:

> I've told you what I see coming. I hope it turns out that I'm wrong, but I don't see how.

The truth is that I *do* see how I could be wrong. After all, like everyone else, I've been wrong before.

And if I've been wrong before, I could be wrong this time. And if I could be wrong this time, I'd be foolish to bet everything I have on being right.

As to whether I *hope* I'm wrong, the answer is most certainly *yes*. And I'm not being coy when I say that. I enjoy prosperity and freedom much more than I would enjoy the fame of a prophet.

I love the blessings of a prosperous economy that makes computers, VCRs, and fax machines better and cheaper with every passing year. I love living in a society that can afford to produce live operas and market videotapes of them. Name anything that comes with prosperity, and there's a good chance that I savor it. I've enjoyed the prosperity of the 1980s as much as you have, and I don't like the thought of giving it up.

I wouldn't want to have to remember to take my ration book when I go to the supermarket. Nor would I enjoy waiting in gasoline lines, or having to provide a good reason for withdrawing money from my bank account.

Less Freedom

And my imagination extends beyond the economic time bomb to the political events that could follow its explosion. I don't expect the government to take the blame for what it has caused.

More likely, the crises will be blamed on you and me. Free enterprise (which will be called "greed"), competition ("economics of the jungle"), open markets ("unlevel playing fields"), and low tax rates for all ("subsidies for the rich") will be attacked as the causes of the crises. We'll be told that letting people make their own economic decisions is "economic violence"—a practice that must be suppressed.

After all the Congressional hearings and the emergency edicts, we'll be far less free to live our lives as we want to.

The American Welfare State was born in the depths of the Great Depression. Italy gladly accepted Mussolini's fascism as a way to end the bread lines and street riots of the early 1920s. And Adolf Hitler's socialism was the welcome answer to Germany's economic devastation.

These may seem to be extreme examples. But think back to the recent election campaign. How many of the solutions offered for economic problems would have *increased* your freedom? The candidates kept your eyes focused on the miraculous benefits, but every new program would take another bite out of your freedom and your property.

We long ago reached the point at which government's grand solutions took precedence over personal freedom. In the midst of another Great Depression, would any politician let your freedom or the sanctity of what you've earned get in the way of his so terribly urgent program?

Yes, I'll be *very* happy if the time bomb doesn't explode. You won't hate me, and we both will be better off.

You'll have a sound portfolio *and* a free and prosperous world in which to enjoy it. Because of your portfolio, you'll be able to relax and to delight in the prosperity, while others will have to wonder when it will end—and whether it might end with a crash.

The Economic Time Bomb

But I don't mean to minimize the urgency.

I *am* very concerned about the future. For the first time in many years, I feel a sense of immediate danger about the economy, and I don't want you to be vulnerable.

I hope my urgings have been persuasive. I hope my presentation has been understandable. And I hope that this book has shown you how you can quit worrying about what the future holds.

Thank you for spending this time with me.

I wish you the very best, and I hope your luck is as good as mine.

November 9, 1988   Harry Browne

Appendices

A

Acknowledgments

Terry Coxon edited and re-edited this book. He made suggestions and challenged assumptions, making the book much more than I could have created on my own. Since 1974, he has helped make my writing better, my presentation clearer, and my ideas sounder.

I'm also grateful to Charles Smith and John Chandler, the publishers of my newsletter. Because of them, I've been able to develop my ideas in print over 14 years. Without that forum, this book never would have been born.

Part of the credit for this book goes also to George Witte of St. Martin's Press; Alan Sergy, who helped with the research; my wife Pamela; and my agent Oscar Collier.

A number of people have contributed to my economic education over the years, but probably the three most important influences were Ludwig von Mises, Murray Rothbard, and Henry Hazlitt.

The book was written using a word-processing program in a Hewlett-Packard 9845C computer—a machine that is ten years old but very fast and very efficient. The graphs were prepared with the same computer system.

Futura Press in Austin, Texas, put the graphs into presentable form and composed the tables.

B

Glossary

Here are definitions of many of the terms used in this book, as well as other terms you might come across when dealing with the investment program.

A definition isn't authoritative; its purpose is to make communication more intelligible. In most cases, I've defined a word in the sense that it's generally understood in the investment and economic worlds, or in the sense that I've used it in the text.

A term appearing in **boldface** within a definition is itself defined in the Glossary. Where a more detailed explanation of a term appears elsewhere in this book, the page number is shown here.

Adjustable-rate mortgage: A **mortgage** whose interest rate is adjusted to current market conditions at set intervals, usually every 6 months.

Advisor: Someone who provides advice regarding investments. He may do so as a personal consultant or financial writer, or as a manager of money—such as through a managed account or a mutual fund.

Agency security: A bond or other **debt instrument** issued by an agency of the U.S. government other than the U.S. Treasury Department.

Annuity: A contract, usually with an insurance company, that promises to pay someone a fixed amount periodically (such as monthly or yearly) over a given period of time—usually for the rest of the person's life.

Arbitrage: The purchase of an **asset** in one market accompanied by a simultaneous sale of the same (or a similar) asset in a different market, to take advantage of a difference in price. The arbitrage principle can be applied to simultaneous buying and selling of related **currencies,** commodities, or **securities;** or the same commodity for different delivery dates. An arbitrager (or arbitrageur) makes such pairs of trades if he believes that one price is likely to change in relation to the other.

Ask price: The price at which a **dealer** is willing to sell to his customers.

Asset: Anything owned on which a value can be placed.

Bag: In **junk silver coin** investments, the basic unit of trading. It is composed of 10,000 dimes, 4,000 quarters, or 2,000 half-dollars—in other words, coins whose **face value** totals $1,000.

Balance: Diversification of investments to prevent being vulnerable to the fortunes of any one.

Balance sheet: A financial statement that lists a firm's or individual's **assets, liabilities,** and **capital** (definition #1).

Bank holiday: A period during which banks are legally permitted to deny, or forced by the government to deny, withdrawal requests from depositors.

Bank run: An epidemic of withdrawal requests motivated by doubts about a bank's solvency.

Banknote: Currency in paper form, as opposed to a bank deposit.

Bankruptcy: The inability to pay debts or other obligations. Also, a formal recognition of that inability.

Bear market: A period during which a price is moving generally downward.

Bearer instrument: Any certificate of ownership (**stock, bond,** note, etc.) that isn't **registered** or made payable to a specific name—and thus is effectively owned by whoever possesses it (the "bearer" of the certificate).

Beta: A measure of a **stock**'s **volatility** and its tendency to move in harmony with stocks in general. A beta of 1.0 indicates (a) a stock that always moves in the same direction, and to the same extent, as the general stock market; or (b) a stock that merely tends to move in the same direction as the general market but also tends to be more volatile. A beta higher than 1.0 indicates that the stock tends to move in the same direction as the market and is more volatile than the average. A beta lower than 1.0 (but greater than 0) means the direction of the stock's movement corresponds to some degree with the general market, but may be less volatile. A negative beta means the stock tends to move in the opposite direction from the general market.

Bid price: The price at which a **dealer** is willing to buy from his customers.

Bill: A short-term debt, usually of no more than 12 months' duration, paying no interest until its **maturity**. (See also **Treasury securities**.)

Blue-chip stock: The **stock** of a large, well-known, financially sound company.

Bond: A **debt instrument** issued by a corporation or government, on which periodic interest payments are made (usually twice yearly), and whose **face value** is payable in full on the **maturity** date.

Borrowing short, lending long: Usually in reference to a bank, the practice of making long-term loans with money provided to the bank by short-term deposits. (See also **Mismatching maturities**.)

Bottom: A price level below any reached during some period of time following.

Broker: One who acts only as a middleman between buyers and sellers; unlike a **dealer**, he doesn't buy and sell for his own account. (Some firms act both as brokers and as dealers.)

Bull market: A period during which the price trend is upward.

Bullion: Bars of refined gold, silver, or other precious metal.

Bullion coin: A coin of gold, silver, or platinum that normally sells at a price close to the value of the metal in the coin. (See pages 174–176.)

Call option: The right to purchase a specified **investment** at a specified price on a specified date or, in some cases, any time prior to a specified date.

Capital: [1] The **net assets** of a person or firm. [2] The sum of money paid into a company by its shareholders.

Capital appreciation or **capital gain:** A profit made from a change in the price of an **investment**.

Cartel: An agreement between governments or companies to limit competition, limit production, or maintain a common price.

Cash: [1] In investment terms, money in coin, **banknotes**, checking accounts, or other **liquid** forms. [2] **Cash equivalents**. [3] Coins or paper **banknotes** alone. [4] Paid for without credit.

Cash equivalent: A liquid investment with a nearly constant dollar value (such as a Treasury bill, savings account, certificate of deposit, and so on) that is held in place of **cash**.

Cash-value life insurance: Life insurance that, in addition to paying benefits in the event of death, accumulates value that the owner can borrow or withdraw from the policy.

CD: Certificate of deposit.

Certificate of deposit: A bank deposit represented by a certificate that is transferable.

CH: The international postal abbreviation for Switzerland (the Confederation of Helvetia); it appears in a Swiss address just before the postal zone number.

Chart: A graph that plots an investment price or economic indicator over a period of time.

Claim account: A financial account representing the right to receive a commodity—as opposed to ownership of the commodity itself. (See page 206.)

Closed-end investment company: A company that invests its stockholders' money in **securities**, and that does not continually **redeem** (buy back) existing shares (as a **mutual fund** does). Its shares are traded in the open market. It is also called a *publicly traded investment fund.*

Collateral: An **asset** that is pledged for a loan, to be sold for the benefit of the lender if repayment is not made.

Collectible: An article valued for its artistic merit, natural beauty, rarity, or historical associations. (See page 187.)

Commercial paper: A **marketable**, short-term **debt instrument**, usually for $100,000 or more, of a well-known corporation.

Compounding: The process of reinvesting **interest, dividends**, or profits at the same rate of return as they earned—allowing them to multiply, rather than simply add to the result.

Consumer Price Index (CPI): An index constructed from the prices of several hundred products and services sold in the U.S., meant to give an indication of the general level of U.S. consumer prices. The **inflation** rate is derived by measuring changes in the CPI. For example, if inflation is said to be 5.0%, it means that the CPI has risen by 5% from its level 12 months earlier.

Consumption: [1] The use or enjoyment of a product or service as an end in itself, rather than as a means to a further end. [2] The using up of something.

Content: The precious metal in a coin, medallion, or token—usually expressed as a number of troy ounces—and disregarding any other metals contained in the coin.

Coupon-equivalent yield: The **yield** of a **Treasury bill** expressed as the yield that a **bond** would have to pay in order to provide the same return. If the bond will make a coupon interest payment before the **maturity** of the T-bill, the interest can be compounded to increase the return; thus a bond requires a lower nominal yield than a T-bill in order to provide the same return.

Coupon rate: The annual rate of interest, expressed as a percentage of the **face value**, paid by a **bond**. (See page 179.)

Creditor: Someone to whom money is owed.

Currency: [1] A brand of **money**, usually created by a government or a **central bank**. [2] **Banknotes** and coins, as opposed to bank deposits.

Custodial account: A **safekeeping account**.

Custodian: An agent, usually a bank, that stores investments.

Custody account: A **safekeeping account**.

Dealer: One who is available either to buy or sell a given investment, as the customer wishes, usually at quoted prices; unlike a **broker**, he owns the investments he offers to sell.

Debt instrument: A **bill**, note, **mortgage**, debenture, **bond**, or other promise to repay a debt.

Default: Failure to keep a promise.

Deferral: See **Tax deferral**.

Deferred annuity: An **annuity** that promises to begin making payments at a future time.

Deficit: The amount by which outgo exceeds income.

Deflation: A fall in the general price level—caused by a growth in the **demand for money** that isn't offset by a comparable growth in the **money supply**, or caused by a decline in the supply of money that isn't offset by a decline in the demand for money. Deflations, especially those occurring abruptly, have sometimes been accompanied by stock-market crashes and **depressionary** business conditions. (See also **Inflation, Disinflation**, and **Consumer Price Index**.)

Demand deposit: A bank deposit that can be withdrawn without penalty at any time (on demand).

Demand for money: The portion of a person's wealth that he wants to hold in the form of **money**. Or the aggregate of the individual demands for money for an entire population.

Demand loan or **demand note:** A loan or note that is payable whenever the **creditor** demands it.

Depreciation: [1] A loss of value. [2] A system for estimating loss of value over time according to a fixed schedule. [3] A reserve fund that facilitates the replacement of an **asset** when it wears out.

Depression: A prolonged period of declining standards of living.

Designated percentage: The percentage of a **Permanent Portfolio** assigned to each investment. The annual **portfolio adjustment**

will cause some of the investment to be bought or sold in order to restore the investment to this share of the overall portfolio.

Devaluation: A government's dishonoring of its promise to **redeem** (definition #2) its **currency** at a stated rate of exchange, lowering the currency's value in relationship to gold or other currencies. (A devaluation can't occur during a time of **floating-exchange rates**, because there is no promise to dishonor when rates are floating.)

Discount: [1] The amount by which an **asset** is priced under its **face value** (or book value), or under the price of another asset that is comparable in some way. [2] The amount by which a **forward price** is below the **spot price**. [3] The amount by which a coin is priced below the value of its metallic **content**. (See also **Premium.**) [4] (verb) To allow for anticipated events when valuing an investment. It is assumed that the present price of an investment already allows for the possibility of future events that are widely anticipated; thus the market is said to "discount" the future.

Disinflation: A slowdown in the rate of **inflation**, without turning into **deflation**. (See also **Consumer Price Index.**)

Diversification: Combining investments that respond differently to economic conditions.

Dividend: Money or other assets distributed by a company to its **shareholders**, usually out of profits.

Divisibility: The capability of being divided into smaller parts. For example, 100 shares of stock are divisible because the owner can sell 60 shares and keep 40; a gold coin is not divisible because the owner cannot break the coin without changing its character.

Dow-Jones Industrial Average: An index reflecting the prices of 30 **blue-chip stocks**; its changes indicate the direction of the market for stocks of large companies.

Economic time bomb: A metaphor for the economic problems that have remained relatively unnoticed but that may explode into financial crises. (See page 11.)

Equity: The current market value of an **investment**, minus all claims against it (from creditors or option holders).

Equity investment: An **investment** that does not promise to pay a specific number of dollars to the investor.

Eurocurrency: A deposit in a bank located outside the country in which the **currency** of the account was issued (such as a U.S. dollar account in a Swiss bank or a Swiss franc account in an English bank).

Exchange control: A government regulation restricting or prohibiting the exporting or importing of **banknotes,** bank deposits, or other monetary instruments.

Exchange rate: The price of one country's **currency** expressed in units of another country's currency.

Exports: Products manufactured in this country and sold outside the country.

Face value: [1] The amount promised to a lender at the **maturity** of a **bond,** note, or **bill.** (See page 179.) [2] The **legal tender** value of a coin, **banknote,** or other token.

FDIC: The Federal Deposit Insurance Corporation, the agency of the U.S. government responsible for reimbursing deposits, up to $100,000, that are lost in bank failures.

Fed: The **Federal Reserve System**.

Federal Reserve System: A system of 12 Federal Reserve Banks, supervised by a Board of Governors, that acts as a central bank in the U.S., and that sets **reserve** requirements and other regulations for commercial banks.

FSLIC: The Federal Savings and Loan Insurance Corporation, the agency of the U.S. government responsible for reimbursing deposits, up to $100,000, that are lost in failures of savings and loan associations.

Fineness: The degree of purity of a bar of **bullion** or a coin, expressed as a decimal fraction. Gold bullion is usually of .995 fineness, which means that 99.5% of the total weight is pure gold. The stated gold weight of a coin or bar of bullion includes only the weight of the gold, disregarding any base metal (such as copper) and impurities, and thus it isn't usually necessary to know the fineness.

Fixed-rate mortgage: A **mortgage** for which the interest rate doesn't change.

Floating exchange rate: An exchange rate that is allowed to fluctuate, not influenced by government purchases and sales. A *dirty float* occurs when the government influences the exchange rate through purchases and sales, but does not announce an official, fixed exchange rate; the dirty float has been the exchange rate system used by most governments since 1973.

Foreign exchange rate: See **Exchange rate**.

Forward contract: A contract for delivery of an **asset** in the future at a price determined in the present.

Forward price: The price of an **asset** to be delivered and paid for on a given date in the future. (See also **Spot price**.)

Free market: Any arrangement for voluntary transactions; an absence of government regulation.

Free trade: An absence of governmental restrictions on the exchange of goods and services. (See also **Protectionism**.)

Fundamental analysis: A method of investment analysis that considers only those sources of supply and demand that are independent of investment opinions. (See also **Technical analysis**.)

Fundamental value: The value an investment appears to have that's separate from what investors may think of it.

Fungible: Interchangeable. For example, shares of stock in General Motors are fungible because any one share is a perfect substitute for any other. Fungible storage of, for instance, gold coins is storage in which no distinction is made as to which owner owns which coins. In non-fungible storage (or **segregated storage**), each coin is attributed to a specific owner.

Futures contract: A **forward contract** with standardized specifications, traded on an organized exchange.

Gold content: See **Content**.

Gram: The basic unit of weight in the metric system. There are 31.1035 grams to a **troy ounce**; 1 gram equals .03215 troy ounce. A kilogram is 1,000 grams or 32.15 troy ounces. A metric ton is 1,000 kilograms, 1,000,000 grams, or 32,151 troy ounces.

Gross national product (GNP): The estimated value of all goods and services produced in a country during a given period of time.

Hard-money investments: Gold and silver, because these metals have served as money that isn't dependent upon the actions of a government. The designation sometimes includes currencies, such as the Swiss franc, that have been subjected to less than average **monetary inflation**.

Hedge: An **investment** purchased to offset possible loss in another investment.

High-grade: Involving a minimum of risk.

Hyperinflation: Runaway inflation.

Ideal Plan: The investment program an individual would select if all his wealth were in **cash**. (See page 225.)

Illiquidity: For an **investment,** the absence of a market in which the investment can be resold easily without paying a penalty for haste.

Imports: Products manufactured outside the country and sold here.

Income (investment): Dividends or **interest** received from an **investment**.

Index futures: See **Stock index futures**.

Indicator (investment): A statistic that is meant to describe the state of an investment or an investment market, or to reveal the future direction of either, or a formula for computing such a statistic.

Individual Retirement Account (IRA): A type of tax-sheltered **pension plan,** not sponsored by an employer, funded by an employee's voluntary contributions.

Inflation: A rise in the general level of consumer prices—caused by a depreciation of the value of **money,** resulting from an increase in the **money supply** that isn't offset by a corresponding increase in the **demand for money**.

Insider trading: Making investments based on information not readily available to the public.

Interest: Payments made to compensate a lender for the use of his capital.

Interest expense: Annual outlays for interest to service existing debt.

Investing: The attempt to earn **income** or profit by making your capital available to an investment market—accepting the return this market offers to everyone. (See page 140, and see also **Speculating.**)

Investment: An **asset** that is purchased in order to profit from the **income** it provides or from an increase in the asset's price.

Investment analysis: A systematic application of principles and rules in an attempt to derive opinions about investments from information available. (See also **Fundamental analysis** and **Technical analysis.**)

Investment company: A company that places its stockholders' money in investments (usually in **securities**).

IRA: Individual Retirement Account.

Junk silver coins: U.S. coins (dimes, quarters, and half-dollars) minted prior to 1965 and containing 90% silver, or half-dollars minted 1965 through 1970 and containing 40% silver, and having no **numismatic** value. (See also **Bag.**)

Keogh plan: A tax-sheltered **pension plan** for self-employed individuals and partnerships.

Kilogram: See **Gram.**

Leverage: Any arrangement (such as a **margin** purchase or an **option** contract) that exaggerates the effect of any change in the price of the **underlying investment**. By analogy, **volatility**.

Liability: A financial obligation.

Limited partnership: A partnership in which some of the partners (the "limited partners") don't participate in management, and aren't liable for the partnership's obligations beyond the amount they have invested.

Liquid asset: An **asset** that can be sold quickly without paying a penalty for haste.

Liquidation: [1] The sale of an **asset**. [2] The closing out or winding down of a company, **annuity**, **pension plan**, or other **investment** or enterprise.

Liquidity: [1] The ability to turn an **asset** into **cash** quickly without a penalty for haste. [2] The relationship of a firm's **liquid assets** to the **liabilities** that might have to be paid in the near future.

Listed option: A **call option** or **put option** that is traded (listed) on an organized exchange.

Load: A sales charge imposed on the purchase of **shares** of a **mutual fund**. (See also **Low-load** and **No-load**.)

Low-load: A sales charge of 2% or less imposed on the purchase of **shares** of a **mutual fund**.

Margin account: An investment account whose assets are used as **collateral** to secure a loan. An investor might borrow money against his investments in order to purchase a greater quantity than would be possible on a cash basis, or to raise cash without selling investments.

Market: [1] A place where (or an arrangement whereby) investors meet to buy and sell a particular investment. [2] An opportunity to exchange.

Market value: The price at which an **asset** can be sold.

Matching maturities: For a bank, matching the **maturities** of loans to the maturities of the deposits that finance the loans.

Maturity: The date on which a contractual obligation (such as repayment of a **bond**) falls due.

Metals account: At a Swiss bank, a **claim account**.

Metric ton: See **Gram**.

Minimum wage law: A law that designates a minimum wage level, below which no worker may be hired and paid.

Mismatching maturities: Making loans of **maturities** that are longer than the maturities of the deposits that finance the loans. (See also **Borrowing short, lending long**).

Monetary cycles: Periods of rapid growth in an economy's **money supply** alternating with periods of very slow growth. Monetary cycles may result in alternating periods of inflation and recession. The "cycles" do not have a fixed length.

Monetary inflation: An increase in the money supply.

Money: Any instrument that is immediately acceptable as a medium of exchange.

Money market fund: A **mutual fund** that invests only in **money-market instruments**.

Money market instrument: An easily **marketable** short-term note or bill carrying little risk of **default**.

Money supply: All of the money (by whatever definition) held by the public. In practice, several definitions of the money supply (known as M_1, M_2, and so on) are referred to in calculating monetary statistics.

Moratorium: A period during which a debtor (such as a bank, company, or individual) is legally permitted to delay payment of his obligations.

Mortgage: A loan that uses real estate as collateral.

Municipal bond: A **bond** issued by a state or city government, or by an agency of a state or city government.

Mutual fund: A company that invests its shareholders' money in other **investments** (usually **securities**) and agrees to **redeem** (buy back) its shares at **net asset value** upon request of the shareholder.

Net assets: Total **assets** minus total **liabilities**.

Net asset value per share: **Net assets** of an **investment company** divided by the number of shares outstanding.

Net worth: Total **assets** minus total **liabilities**.

New money: Additions to the **money supply**.

Newsletter: A periodical, available through mail subscription only, designed to provide news and advice regarding a specific subject—such as investments.

No-load: With no commission imposed when purchasing a **mutual fund**. (See also **Load** and **Low-load**.)

Non-problem: In the context of this book, an economic issue or other matter that is commonly perceived to be a problem, but is not considered so by the author.

Numismatic coin: A coin that has substantial value in excess of its metallic **content**.

Odd lot: An investment transaction that is smaller than the customary minimum transaction. An odd-lot transaction may be subject to additional charges.

Option: See **Call option** and **Put option.**

Ordinary income: Interest, dividends, rents, royalties, income from annuities, and income from employment or a business.

Paper promise: An **investment,** such as a **security,** that relies for its value on the promise of its issuer to make payments in the future.

Paper money: Money in the form of **banknotes** or bank deposits. Historically, the expression refers to money that isn't convertible into gold.

Par: [1] See **Par value.** [2] Equal in value.

Par value: The nominal or **face value** of a **security** or **currency.**

Peak: A price level above any reached during some period of time following.

Pension plan: A legal arrangement for holding **investments** that allows the **income** and profits from investments to accumulate tax-free until money is withdrawn from the plan.

Permanent Portfolio: A **balanced** collection of investments whose structure is meant to remain unchanged from year to year. (See page 144, and see also **Variable Portfolio.**)

Portfolio: A collection of **investments.**

Portfolio adjustment: For a **Permanent Portfolio,** sales and purchases of investments in order to restore each investment's share of the portfolio to its **designated percentage.** (See page 163.)

Premium: [1] The amount by which a **security** is priced above its **face value,** book value, or the value of its component parts. [2] The amount by which a **forward price** exceeds the **spot price.** [3] The amount by which the price of a coin exceeds the value of the coin's metallic **content.** [4] The amount by which the price of an **option** exceeds its exercise value (colloquially, "premium" often means the entire price of the option). [5] The payment required to keep an insurance policy in force.

Price controls: Laws that designate a maximum price (or a minimum price) that may be charged for a product or service.

Price inflation: An increase in the general price level.

Program trading: The use of computer programs to determine when to buy and sell **investments**.

Protectionism: Governmental restrictions on the international exchange of products and services. The term normally refers to restrictions on products and services coming into a country. (See also **Free trade** and **Tariff**.)

Public market: An investment **market** in which most relevant information is publicly available, and to which any investor has access.

Publicly traded investment fund: A **closed-end investment company**.

Purchasing power: The value of a unit of **money** or other **asset** measured by the goods and services it can purchase. The purchasing power value of an investment normally is calculated by adjusting the investment's price in accordance with changes in the U.S. **Consumer Price Index**.

Put option: The right to sell a specified **investment** at a specified price on a specified date or, in some cases, any time prior to a specified date.

Ratio scale: A graphic scale in which any given percentage difference between prices will cover the same vertical distance, no matter at what level it occurs. For example, the physical distance on the graph between 40 and 60 will be the same as between 100 and 150, because both intervals represents an increase of 50%. On a *linear scale,* the physical distance between 100 and 150 (the difference between which is 50) will be 2½ times as great as that between 40 and 60 (the difference between which is 20).

Recession: A period during which the level of economic activity declines.

Redeem: See **Redemption**.

Redemption: [1] The repurchase of a **security** by its issuer—usually the repurchase of its shares by a **mutual fund** upon request of the shareholder. [2] The conversion of a **currency** into gold or silver by the currency's issuer.

Registered security: A **security** whose ownership is recorded with the issuer.

Regulation: Government rules that restrict commercial or financial activities.

Repo: Repurchase agreement.

Repurchase agreement: A contract under which an **investment** is sold by one party to another with the stipulation that it be repurchased on a specified date at a specified (higher) price. It is, in effect, a loan of money using the investment as **collateral**, with the difference in the two prices representing the **interest**.

Reserve: [1] An allocation of **capital** for possible losses or to meet a legal requirement. [2] For a bank, the money available to meet withdrawal requests.

Reserve Bank: One of 12 banks comprising the **Federal Reserve System**.

Risk: The possibility of loss and the extent of the potential loss.

Round lot: The customary minimum size of an investment transaction—number of shares of stock, for example.

Runaway inflation: A rapid increase in prices aggravated by a widespread drop in the **demand for money**.

Safekeeping account: An account by which a bank stores property belonging to the customer.

Security: [1] A **stock, bond,** or investment contract. [2] **Collateral**. [3] Safety.

Segregated storage: Storage of an asset in such a way that it can be identified as belonging solely to a particular person.

Selling short: See **Short sale**.

Short sale: [1] The sale of a **security** or other **asset** an investor has borrowed. The short-seller will have to purchase the asset eventually in order to repay what he has borrowed; thus he profits from a fall in the asset's price. [2] The sale of an asset for future delivery. If the seller does not own the asset now, he is betting that he will be able to acquire the asset before the delivery date at a lower price than that at which he has sold it.

Soft landing: An end to **price inflation** not accompanied by either a **depression** or **runaway inflation**.

Speculating: An attempt to exceed the gains achievable through investing—by careful timing of investments, by selection of individual stocks, or by attempting to outwit the market in any other way. (See page 140, and see also **Investing**.)

Speculative: In conventional usage, involving more than a minimum of **risk**. (See also **Speculating**.)

Spot price: The price for immediate delivery of an **asset**. (See also **Forward price**.)

Spread: [1] The difference between the **bid price** and the **ask price**. (See page 176.) [2] A type of **hedge** or **arbitrage** involving the purchase of an **asset** for delivery on one date and the sale of the same asset for delivery on a different date. [3] The simultaneous buying of one commodity or financial instrument and the selling of another, in order to profit from an expected change in the price relationship between the two. It is sometimes called a *straddle*.

Stability: An absence of fluctuations. The opposite of **volatility**.

Stock: An ownership interest in the net **income** and net **assets** of a corporation.

Stock index futures: A **futures contract** whose value depends on the movement in a stock index (such as the Standard & Poor's 500 index). It must be sold and settled by a designated expiration date.

Stockpile: An existing inventory.

Stop-loss order: An instruction given to a bank or **broker** to sell an **investment** if the price drops to a stated level.

Strategy: A plan or program that provides guidelines for achieving a given objective.

Supply of money: See **Money supply**.

System (investment): A trading program that generates buy and sell instructions automatically, usually by reading one or more **indicators**.

Tariff: A tax applied to **imports**.

Tax deferral: The delaying of the date when income will be recognized for tax purposes.

Tax-exempt: Free of taxation. The interest on a **municipal bond**

is exempt from federal income tax, while the interest on **Treasury securities** is exempt from state and local taxation.

Tax shelter: An **investment** or arrangement that legally provides **tax deferral** or tax reduction.

T-bills: U.S. Treasury bills. (See **Treasury securities**.)

Technical analysis: A system of investment analysis that considers factors relating to supply and demand only within the investment market without regard for **fundamental values**. (See also **Fundamental analysis**.)

Tight money: A slowdown in the creation of new money by the **Federal Reserve System**.

Time deposit: A nontransferable bank deposit that is not withdrawable until a fixed date.

Ton, metric: 1,000,000 **grams** or 1,000 kilograms.

Top: An investment price that isn't reached again for a substantial period of time.

Track record: Record of performance. For an **advisor**, the gains or losses achieved by actual or hypothetical accounts for which he has chosen the investments.

Trade balance: The value of a nation's **exports** minus the value of its **imports**.

Trade deficit: A negative **trade balance**.

Transaction costs: Commissions, **spreads** (definition #1), or other costs incurred in buying and selling **investments**.

Treasury securities: Debts that are direct obligations of the U.S. government. They include Treasury **bills** (maturing within one year after they are issued), Treasury notes (maturing between 1 and 10 years after issue), and Treasury **bonds** (maturing more than 10 years after issue).

Troy ounce: The unit of weight used to measure gold and silver. One troy ounce equals 1.097 avoirdupois ounces—the weight used in the U.S. for commercial and household purposes.

Trust: An entity created and financed by one person (the grantor) for the benefit, usually, of another person (the **beneficiary**), and controlled by a third person (the **trustee**).

Trustee: The entity, often a bank, who controls a **trust** and is usually empowered to buy and sell investments for the trust.

Underlying investment: The **investment** that can be purchased or sold on specified terms by the holder of an **option, warrant,** or other convertible security.

Variable annuity: An **annuity** whose value depends upon the performance of a pool of **investments**.

Variable life insurance: An insurance policy, the cash value of which depends upon the performance of a pool of **investments.**

Variable Portfolio: A collection of **investments** that is altered as investment prospects change. It should be funded only with money you can afford to lose. (See page 145, and see also **Permanent Portfolio.**)

Volatility: The tendency of an **investment**'s price to fluctuate. The opposite of **stability.**

Warrant: An option to purchase a share of stock at a specified price until a specified date. A warrant differs from a **call option** in that a warrant is issued by the company whose stock is involved.

Yield: An **investment**'s **interest** or **dividend** stated as a percentage of the investment's current **market value.** For example, a bond paying $90 per year interest and selling for $900 has a yield of 10%.

Zero-coupon bond: A **bond** that earns **interest** but does not pay it until **maturity.** A zero-coupon bond accumulates and **compounds** interest, so that all interest earnings are reinvested at the same interest rate that prevailed when the bond was bought.

C

_____

Explanations of Graphs

$\mathbf{T}$his appendix provides background information for the graphs and tables appearing in the book.

Price Inflation (page 27)

Changes in the yearly average of the U.S. Consumer Price Index (CPI).

Data are estimates of the U.S. Bureau of Labor Statistics. From 1913, they are from the Consumer Price Index for Urban Wage Earners and Clerical Workers. For the years prior to 1913, they are reconstructed estimates, and they appear in *Historical Statistics of the United States, Colonial Times to 1970* (U.S. Department of Commerce, page 211, series E135). The 1988 CPI was estimated to be the average between June and July 1988.

Consumer Prices (page 28)

Yearly averages of the absolute value of the U.S. Consumer Price Index—with data from the sources shown for the preceding graph. The data have been adjusted to make 1988 equal to 100, so that you can easily compare the general price level of any prior time to the present.

Money Creation (page 30)

The yearly change in the U.S. money supply (M2 definition).

Data for 1960–1988 are the latest versions provided by the Federal Reserve System.

Data for 1949–1959 were taken from *Historical Statistics of the United States, Colonial Times to 1970* (U.S. Department of Commerce, pages 992–993, series X414), and were originally estimated by Milton Friedman and Anna Jacobson Schwartz for their book, *A Monetary History of the United States, 1867–1960.* These figures were adjusted to make them consistent with the 1960–1988 data.

Bank Failures (page 48)

The yearly total number of banks closed because of financial difficulties, plotted through 1987. The data are taken from the *Federal Deposit Insurance Corporation 1987 Annual Report* (table 122, page 49).

U.S. Trade Balance (page 101)

The merchandise trade balance of the United States, expressed as a percentage of each year's Gross National Product (GNP).

The trade data for 1790–1970 are taken from *Historical Statistics of the United States, Colonial Times to 1970* (U.S. Department of Commerce, pages 866–868, series U15). Data for 1971–1987 are taken from *Economic Indicators* (U.S. Government Printing Office, various issues, Merchandise Net Balance).

The Gross National Product data for 1870–1970 are taken

from *Historical Statistics of the United States, Colonial Times to 1970* (U.S. Department of Commerce; pages 224, 231, and 239; series F1, F71, and F238). Prior to 1889, the plots are at irregular intervals, because data aren't available for every year. Since no GNP data are available for years prior to 1839, I have projected backward the GNP data of later years. Data for 1971–1987 are taken from *Economic Indicators* (U.S. Government Printing Office, various issues, page 1).

For both the trade balance and GNP, 1988 was estimated from data for the first six months.

Stability in a Permanent Portfolio (page 158)

The hypothetical result shown for the Permanent Portfolio is calculated using a portfolio split evenly among four investments: common stocks, gold, Treasury bonds, and Treasury bills.

The value of the portfolio's stocks is calculated by using the New York Stock Exchange Composite Index as a proxy for all stock-market investments. Dividends are assumed to be 4% per year; although this is a low figure, it is in keeping with the use of volatile mutual funds or stocks, which generally have low yields.

The value of the portfolio's gold component is based on the London afternoon gold fixing.

The value of the portfolio's bond component is based on an index derived from 20-year and 30-year Treasury bond yields reported by the Federal Reserve. The interest paid is assumed to be 8% of the face value, which provides a different yield each year—depending on the value of the bond index.

The value of the portfolio's Treasury bills is based on the assumption that 52-week bills are purchased on the first day of the calendar year, and the yield prevailing on January 1 is spread throughout the year.

The portfolio is calculated and plotted for each Friday. A portfolio adjustment (as described on page 163) is made on the final Friday of each year.

Transaction costs of 2% to buy and 2% to sell are applied to all the portfolio's investments at the outset, and to all transactions required by portfolio adjustments.

The three investments shown separately are the New York Stock Exchange Composite Index, the London afternoon gold fixing, and an index based on 20-year and 30-year Treasury bond yields reported by the Federal Reserve. Each has been adjusted to be equal to 100 on January 1, 1970. No dividends or interest are included in their calculations, because the plot lines are meant to show merely whether each investment's price was rising or falling at any particular time.

The last date plotted is June 24, 1988.

Value of the Portfolio Adjustment (page 166)

The adjusted portfolio is exactly the same as that described for the preceding graph, adjusted on the final Friday of each year. The unadjusted portfolio begins with the same investment distribution but receives no portfolio adjustments.

Index

The Author

Harry Browne is an investment advisor, the author of eight books prior to this one, a newsletter writer, and a public speaker.

He was born in New York City in 1933, but grew up in Los Angeles. He has since lived in Vancouver, Canada, and Zürich, Switzerland. He now resides in Northern California with his wife, Pamela.

His first book was *How You Can Profit from the Coming Devaluation* (1970). His most popular books have been *You Can Profit from a Monetary Crisis* (1974) and *How I Found Freedom in an Unfree World* (1973), a non-investment book that continues to be in demand today.

In addition, he has written *The Complete Guide to Swiss Banks* (1976), *New Profits from the Monetary Crisis* (1978), *Inflation-Proofing Your Investments* (1981, with Terry Coxon), *Investment Rule #1* (1985), and *Why the Best-Laid Investment Plans Usually Go Wrong* (1987).

Since 1974, he has been writing *Harry Browne's Special Reports,* a financial newsletter published eight to ten times yearly.

His other interests include classical music, opera, German operetta, playing the piano, good food, wine, sports, television, and other forms of fiction.